DICTIONARY OF CUMBRIAN DIALECT, TRADITION AND FOLKLORE

Dictionary

of
Cumbrian
Dialect, Tradition and Folklore

William Rollinson
MA, PhD, FRGS

Illustrated by Peter Kearney

Smith
Settle

First published in 1997 by

Smith Settle Ltd
Ilkley Road
Otley
West Yorkshire
LS21 3JP

ISBN   Paperback   1 85825 066 8
       Hardback   1 85825 067 6

British Library Cataloguing-in-Publication Data:
A catalogue record is available for this book
from the British Library.

Set in ITC Stone Informal & Stone Sans

Designed, printed and bound by
SMITH SETTLE
Ilkley Road, Otley, West Yorkshire LS21 3JP

For Tony and Marjory Trohear

Acknowledgements

My sincere thanks are due to the following:

Michael Moon, Pat Jones, Arthur Evans, Dr Christopher Carter, the late Muriel Smalley, Jack Kellet, Dr David Shotter, Jean Scott-Smith, Barbara Trescatheric, Ted Relph, Ron Smith, Jean Crouch, Patrick Duff Pennington, George Bott, Tony Trohear

Christine Denmead drew the frontispiece map and proofread the manuscript with her usual eagle eyes, but if any errors remain they are entirely my fault. Finally, a special word of thanks to Peter Kearney who produced such splendid line drawings, and to Melvyn Bragg for writing the foreword and for his valuable comments.

Foreword

by
Melvyn Bragg

I have thoroughly enjoyed browsing through this *Cumbrian Dictionary* and I have no doubt whatsoever that I will return and refer to it, constantly. In a handy volume, William Rollinson provides a powerful package; dialect, folklore, traditions, local biographies, local customs, glimpses of history and romance, and the overall sense of a sturdy locality which was already in the fells and on the plains over a thousand years ago.

British history and the unfolding of our language and customs is as vivid, passionate, quirky and remarkable as any I can think of. The same applies to the different regions in Britain and the Cumbrian region can make a fair claim to play a distinctive role. Inside this dialect dictionary is a fine sense of how we got from the past to the present. This book is not meant to be a history and its prime purpose as a dictionary of dialect, tradition and folklore is fully achieved. But for those with any sense of previous generations, these words and their associations give an insight into a part of Britain spectacular in scenery and soldiery, and yielding up more than its far share of saints, scholars, artists, scientists and eccentrics. Cumbria has much to boast about and in these well-illustrated pages I think you will find surprise and delight at the range of mind and matter which has thrived in the sparsely populated acres of the Northern regions.

When I submitted my first novel — *For Want of a Nail* — in 1964, the London publisher was worried about the look of the dialect on the page. No one would understand it, he said. I spoke it aloud and he retreated a little but only a little. It is, or has become, a spoken and not a nationally written form — to its great disadvantage.

This is unfortunate, I think. There is a body of fine dialect, poetry and stories, and yet they seem confined to the area as if to let them out would be to cause too many problems.

Given the odds against the dialect over the centuries it is a miracle that it survived so long and so strongly. I regret that I did not push harder for more dialect in the 60s but that was the time of new television standardisation; American/English was gathering force and the dialects began to be left behind.

A book such as this is a very necessary counter-attack. It is strange how readily we have absorbed Americanisms and yet resisted words from our own regions.

It seemed that all was lost. But there are hopeful signs of which this is one. *Trainspotting* for instance has brought the Glaswegian/ Scottish dialect into the bestseller list; perhaps a renewed faith in our own past will spread from there. I hope so. Should that happen, this book will be an invaluable source as well as a continuing pleasure.

Preface

There are many pitfalls involved in writing a book like this one. First, it has to be said that this is not an academic study; those who wish to make a detailed analysis of the Cumbrian dialect should consult the largely nineteenth-century volumes mentioned in the bibliography. Rather it is a companion volume to Dr Arnold Kellett's *The Yorkshire Dictionary of Dialect, Tradition and Folklore*, a forerunner to this present book, and as such is a personal survey of the dialect and folk traditions of Cumbria. Inevitably some readers will find that a favourite word, legend, or anecdote remembered from their youth is missing from this study, and to them I offer my apologies and plead the pressures of trying to get a quart into a pint pot!

Further problems arise with the depiction of dialect on the printed page; not surprisingly, it looks strange since by its very nature it was intended to be spoken rather than read. Melvyn Bragg, himself a fine Cumbrian dialect speaker, puts it graphically:

'It takes a bit of getting used to on paper; it looks very awkward, as if it had forgotten to take off its walking boots and clomped onto the nice clean page too rudely. It demands to be spoken.'

And within Cumbria there are considerable variations in pronunciation and meaning. The Longtown dialect has a Lowland Scottish sound, parts of the north-east of Cumbria have distinct similarities to the Northumbrian dialect, while Barrow, Furness and Cartmel which, until 1974 were part of Lancashire, still retain the loyal toast to the Queen, *Duke* of Lancaster, as well as marked affinities with the Lancastrian dialect. Such regional differences are reflected in certain words; take, for example, the name of the farm building which houses cows — in West Cumbria the term is **coo-as** (cow house) but in North Cumbria the word **byre** is more common, while in the south of the county **shippon** is more frequently used. Similarly, the word **beck**, a small stream, is used throughout most of Cumbria except in the far north where the Scottish term **burn** is encountered. Yet such variety adds to the richness of the Cumbrian dialect.

In deciding which individuals and traditions should be included or excluded, some difficult decisions had to be made. In many instances the decisions were arbitrary, but in others I have been guided by certain principles; figures such as John Peel and William Wordsworth, because of their Cumbrian birth and stature as well as the folk stories which surround them, have been included, but others such as Coleridge, Southey and the rest of the Lakes Poets have not. Prominent off-comers such as Beatrix Potter, Father Thomas West, the writer of the first guidebook to the Lakes, and Alfred Wainwright are included, but writers such as Hugh Walpole and Arthur Ransome have been left out. On the whole I have concentrated on the lesser-known but larger-than-life Cumbrian characters such as Mally Messenger, Peter Crosthwaite, Lanty Slee, Will Ritson, John Wilkinson and Parson Sewell — all of whom feature prominently in fable and folklore. Certain traditions such as **pace-egging**, **knur and spell**, **mummers**, **rush-bearings** and the Arthurian legends are found in neighbouring counties and further afield, but all are an essential part of Cumbrian folk tradition and therefore find a place here.

It should not be assumed that all the words and phrases in this dictionary are currently in use in Cumbria. Fortunately, many can still be heard in cattle marts, at shepherds' meets, at hound trails and in rural pubs, but sadly, the opportunities to hear and speak dialect are diminishing. Despite the efforts of the Lakeland Dialect Society, recent research (see pages xvi-xvii) suggests that the knowledge and use of dialect words is declining and, because of the appeal of imported antipodean TV 'soap operas', many Cumbrian children are more familiar with the patois of South East Australia than with the dialect of their **forelders** ...

I hope this book will remind those readers over forty of words and traditions which were once familiar to them and also introduce younger readers to a rich and varied language and folk tradition which is part of their cultural heritage. Almost a century ago, Bryham Kirkby wrote a short introduction to his *Lakeland Words* in which he claimed that his work was an attempt:

'... to present an inside view of the dialect, marred no doubt by the leanings of prejudice, and for its worst defects the only indulgence that is asked is that is that it may be judged with that consideration in mind. It is a lover's account and as such must be excused.'

The present author can merely hope that his efforts will be viewed in the same light.

William Rollinson
Ulverston, Cumbria

Introduction

In a world which has become sanitised and standardised, where creeping uniformity means that High Streets and shopping 'malls' are identical whether they are in Gateshead or Grimsby, Carlisle or Colchester, we are in danger of losing our regional identity. One single characteristic provides a bulwark against this numbing uniformity — the rich and varied sounds of local dialects. Yet, despite the media attention received by some localities — one thinks of Yorkshire (*Emmerdale* and *Last of the Summer Wine*), London's Dockland (*EastEnders*), Liverpool (*Brookside*) and South Lancashire (*Coronation Street*) — many regional dialects are in decline. Few would argue against encouraging children to express themselves fluently in Standard English, but if that also means the exclusion of the unwritten language of dialect, then we will be the poorer for it. Schools have traditionally been the enemy of dialect, yet until relatively recently many children were bilingual, using the 'secret' language of the playground, which often incorporated dialect words, but speaking 'proper' English in the classroom.

Sadly, it has become accepted that somehow dialect is not 'nice', that it is uncouth and raw and must therefore be checked. Indeed, the need to conform has driven thousands of students from northern provincial schools to alter their speech patterns within weeks of 'going up' to university, and after a single term they emerge newly-equipped with pseudo-Standard English in which dialect finds no place. Only when under stress or pressure will the true nature of their origins and background be revealed by a rogue dialect word. At the end of a radio news bulletin during the Second World War, that stalwart Yorkshire broadcaster, Wilfred Pickles, desperately needed to fill in a few seconds; on a spur-of-the-moment impulse he ended his newscast by bidding listeners 'Good neet' — resulting in consternation within the staid, Reithian confines of Broadcasting House in London, but delight and elation throughout the entire North of England! And some readers will recall the furore in the House of Commons several years ago when Prime Minister Thatcher let slip the East Midlands dialect word '*frit*', meaning scared or frightened. Yet there should be no shame or stigma attached to the use of these and similar words which, after all, convey not only meaning but also history.

The Cumbrian Dialect

Although the County of Cumbria was created in 1974 by a 'shotgun marriage' of Cumberland, Westmorland, Lancashire North of the Sands and a small part of Yorkshire, the name is derived from an ancient Celtic word which emerged, phoenix-like, from the so-called Dark Ages when this area of the north-west was originally the land of the Cymry or compatriots, and from the same element the word Cymru, the land of the Celtic Welshmen, emerged. Over the succeeding centuries, despite its local differences, a dialect was forged by Celt, Anglian and Norseman; a tongue which Norman Nicholson has aptly described as a 'clicking, cracking, harshly melodious tune', and which, broadly speaking, distinguishes this region from its neighbours, Scotland, Northumberland, Yorkshire and Lancashire. But the present county boundary must not be considered as a bastion against outside influences; in the north, words such as **sark**, **shoup**, **greetin'** and **lang syne** are used on both sides of the Anglo-Scottish border. In West Cumbria that essentially Northumbrian word **marra** is also an integral part of the dialect, and readers of Arnold Kellett's forerunner to this volume, *The Dictionary of Yorkshire Dialect, Tradition and Folklore*, will appreciate the large number of words which are common to that county and to Cumbria.

Most of the nineteenth century dialect dictionaries concentrate on the rural areas; this is not surprising since these are the most conservative regions, the seed-bed of both dialect and folk tradition. Urban areas such as Carlisle, Whitehaven, Workington, Barrow and Kendal had a greater turn-over of population and were influenced more by **off-comers** — but herein lies another strand of interest. Whitehaven, with its almost complete monopoly of the eighteenth century coal trade with Ireland, was an early magnet for Irish settlers, and this was intensified in the nineteenth century when the linen mill and iron ore mines of the new settlement at Cleator Moor attracted hundreds of Irish immigrants who created a virtual Irish enclave in West Cumbria. In the south of the county, Barrow, that burgeoning, bustling iron and shipbuilding town, drew its workforce from Ireland, Staffordshire, the Black Country, Scotland, and Lancashire as well as from the Cumbrian fells. In the 1870s, attracted by the developing iron mines in Furness, west and south Cumberland, hundreds of Cornish miners and their families flocked into the area; in the case of the village of Roose in Low Furness, they established a Cornish community complete with its chapel dedicated to St Perran. Clearly these migratory movements influenced the local dialect and it comes as no surprise that Barrovians use such a strange mixture of sounds. The idiosyncratic glottal stop which turns water into **wa'er** and bottle into **bo'le** is still noticeable, but even more characteristic is the long Lancashire **oo** sound in 'book' and 'look'. Well might the headmaster of the former Barrow Grammar School for Boys insist, in vain, that **boooks** were **bucks** — but at least one generation of recalcitrant schoolboys were equally adamant that these were either male rabbits or American dollars !

An Historical Survey

Celtic Echoes

Following the collapse of Roman Britain early in the fifth century, the ancient Celtic language re-established itself and, until the eighth century, Cumbria was essentially a Celtic region in which the inhabitants spoke a form of gaelic language understood in Ireland, Scotland, Wales, Cornwall and Brittany. Place-name elements such as *pen* (head) as in Penrith and Penruddock, *blaen* (top) in Blencow and Blencathra, and *glyn* (valley) in Glencoyne and Glenderamakin, are closely related to their Welsh counterparts, and several river names — the Irt, Esk and Kent — are Celtic in origin. The oft-quoted sheep-scoring numerals (page144) provide the best linguistic connection with the 'Celtic twilight', for this seems to have been a method of counting in groups of five, and the words for one, five, ten, fifteen and twenty are remarkably similar in Cumbrian dialect, Old Welsh, Cornish, and the ancient Breton language. Not long ago an enterprising Keswick restaurant owner named his establishment the Yan, Tyan, Tethera — one, two, three in the ancient sheep-scoring numerals; sadly, many visitors mistook it for a Chinese restaurant...!

The Anglian Assimilation

By the last decades of the seventh century, a new group of people began to infiltrate Cumbria from the north-east; these Anglian farmers, seeking out the best quality lands, came over the Pennine passes and settled in the Eden valley, the Solway plain, West Cumbria, the Furness and Cartmel lowlands, and the Kent Valley. Like the Celts, they, too, left their place names — the *-inham*, *-ington* and *-ton* endings bristle on present-day maps, but their influence on dialect was considerable. Old English words such as fluke (*floc*, a flat fish), grave (*grafan*, to dig), frosk (*frosc*, a frog), owt (*awiht*, anything) and gavelock (*gafeluc*, a lever) are some of the many words introduced by these Anglian 'off-comers'. Exactly what became of the native Celts is unclear, though in AD 685 King Ecgfrith of Northumbria granted to St Cuthbert land in Carlisle together with Cartmel 'and all the British therein', which suggests that the Celts were regarded as goods and chattels to be disposed of at will.

The Norse-Irish Influence

The Anglian people undoubtedly influenced Cumbrian dialect, but the subsequent influx of Norse-Irish settlers made the most lasting and significant impact on both the language and folklore. Unlike many other parts of Britain, the Norse people seemed to have arrived in Cumbria not as fierce warriors and raiders but as settlers; moreover, the evidence suggests that they were not pure 'Vikings' but a fusion of Irish and Norse cultures. In the east of England the Viking invaders came mainly from Denmark, but in Cumbria the settlers brought with them, via Ireland and the Isle of Man, a marked Western Norwegian influence, and test-words such as *thwaite, booth, gill, beck* and *foss* — elements which are not common in Denmark — are scotched on the fellsides of Cumbria.

All the Scandinavian languages — Norwegian, Danish, Swedish and Icelandic — are derived from Old Norse which, like Old English, is a Germanic language. Of these, the least changed is Icelandic which bears a very close similarity to Old Norse, the language of the Viking peoples. Even today, children in Iceland can read the sagas in the original language in which they were written. Iceland was settled from AD 874 largely by Norse people from Western Norway, as, indirectly, was Cumbria, so it is not surprising that there is a close affinity between Icelandic and the Cumbrian dialect. The first to recognise the 'Norse Connection' was Thomas de Quincey who, according to that eminent scholar W G Collingwood, advanced 'the line of thought that led to the recognition of the Viking element in the Lake District dialect and place names'. His thesis was further developed in the late nineteenth century by the Rev Thomas Ellwood, Rector of Torver, whose *Lakeland and Iceland* (1895) glossary underlines the close connection between Iceland and Cumbria. But perhaps the most fascinating of all the links is the story related by Canon Sam Taylor in his book *Cartmel People and Priory* (1955) concerning Harold Manning, a Flookburgh man who was posted to Iceland during World War II, and who had found that Icelanders not only understood his home dialect, but when he went fishing with them he had no difficulty in understanding the Icelandic terms they used. I have taken Ellwood's glossary with me on many visits to Iceland and can say with conviction that the Cumbrian dialect is understood there. With that in mind I have, in this dictionary, indicated many words which are identical or very similar to Icelandic and, to a lesser extent, Norwegian.

The Norse influence is apparent not only in dialect but in folklore. Traditions such as fire-cults, and funeral, wedding and Christening customs are similar in the Scandinavian world as well as in Ireland, the Isle of Man and parts of Scotland — all areas colonised by people of Scandinavian extraction.

The Norman Incursion

Apart from one or two locations in the south of the county, Cumbria does not feature in the *Domesday Book* for the simple reason that this remote, isolated area was debateable land, claimed, counter-claimed and fought over by both Scotland and England. Not until 1092, when William ll siezed Carlisle, did the region become part of the English Crown — but not for long. In 1135 most of Cumberland and Westmorland once again became Scottish; in

1157 Henry II regained the area for England, but in 1174 the Scottish king, William the Lion, reinforced his claim by besieging Carlisle for three months. In 1216 Alexander II held the city and the castle until finally this game of political football was brought to a halt by Henry III who bribed Alexander into withdrawing.

All this meant that the Norman hold on Cumbria was not as great as in many other parts of England, and although Norman French was the language of the court and the nobles, almost certainly a type of Norse language was spoken in the fells and Scandinavian culture remained important. The evidence is clear; in 1163 a committee of 'thirty sworn men' witnessed a document which divided the Furness fells between the Abbot of Furness and the Baron of Kendal. Over half of those men were of Scandinavian origin, with names such as Swein, Ravenkell, Ketel, Ulf, Orm and Gospatrick — the latter is clearly a Norse-Irish name.

But even more significant are the several inscriptions in Scandinavian-type runes which indicate that even in the middle of the twelfth century a form of Norse was being written and, by analogy, also spoken. One of the finest is carved on the early medieval font in Bridekirk Church, but there is a remarkable runic inscription on a tympanum stone dating from c1160 in Pennington Church, and even a piece of runic graffiti in Carlisle Cathedral. If the written Norse language survived into the twelfth century, it is not surprising, then, that it should have survived in its dialect form until the twentieth.

The Demise of Dialect?

In a remarkable piece of research initiated by Mrs E R Fieldhouse and followed up by Mr J T Franks, the extent of dialect decline in Furness between 1969 and 1993 has been highlighted. ('The Dialect of Furness', *Journal of the Lakeland Dialect Society*, No 56, 1995.) Some 248 local schoolchildren were questioned in both years. (300 pupils answered the 1966 survey as opposed to 248 in 1993. The scores for 1966 have therefore been reduced so both represent approximately 248 'testees'.) The results are both surprising and depressing, and the use of many words has declined almost to the point of extinction. In the following list the first figure indicates the number of correct answers in 1969, the latter figure refers to 1993:

swill	44/1
lonning	35/3
slape	50/2
shuppon	51/2

Other words fared slightly better:

clarty	44/6
sneck	45/10
lile	50/25
yam	51/27
gauk	40/7

Some words which were quite well known in 1969 scored no marks whatever in 1993; among them were **lish, thrang, yak, kist, laik** and, most surprising of all, **yowe**. Folk traditions rated a remarkably low score in 1993; such erstwhile activities such as **barring out, auld wife hakes, throwing the stocking, whittlegate** and **merry neets** were totally unknown to Furness youngsters in the last decade of the twentieth century — though six recognised a **moonleet flit**... The impact of modern technology and moral values has certainly exerted an influence; when asked to define **hack**, one youngster affirmed that it meant the entering of a computer programme while another claimed it meant a football foul; **crack** was described as a drug, **ken** was a character in *Coronation Street*, and **back-end** was variously described as back-side, rear and bum...! *O Tempora, O Mores!*

Unfortunately the results of the Furness survey seem to be reflected throughout the county and the words of Mrs Fieldhouse in 1969 —'It is expected that quite soon very few traces of the dialect will remain' — have the ring of truth. As with village post offices and rural transport, the message is simple: Use it — or Lose it!

Cumbrian Sounds

The only reliable way in which to determine how Cumbrian dialect is pronounced is to listen to it being spoken. The following is merely a general guide.

Vowels

a the short 'a' before '-ng' in Cumbrian retains the 'a' sound, so ***strang*** (strong), ***lang***, (long) and ***wrang*** (wrong) rhyme with the Standard English 'bang'. The long 'a' in 'late' and 'spade' produces a variety of sounds; in the case of 'spade', in the north-east the vowel has an 'here' sound but in the south an 'ay' sound is more common

i is rather like a short 'ee' sound, but in the north of Cumbria the vowel in such words as 'time' and 'side' becomes an 'ey', ie ***teym*** and ***seyd***

oo in West Cumbria the word 'noon' sounds like ***ni-un*** but in South Cumbria, where the long Lancastrian 'ooo' sound is common, the word becomes an elongated ***nooon*** sound

u words like 'house' and 'now' have an 'oo' vowel in the north of the county but an 'ow' sound in the south

Consonants

d sounds like a soft 'th', as in ***wedder*** (weather) and ***fadder*** (father)

g replaces the Standard English '-dge' sound as in ***brig*** for bridge *gh* the gutteral 'gh' survives in North Cumbria, especially around Carlisle, but elsewhere it is not particularly common

h words beginning with 'h' normally retain that letter through most of central and northern Cumbria, but in the south the dropping of the 'h' is common, so 'him' becomes *'im* and 'how' becomes *'ow*

k in the Cumbrian dialect this often represents the 'ch' of Standard English and is probably a result of the Scandinavian influence. 'Birch' therefore becomes *birk* (ON *björk*), 'church' becomes *kirk* (ON *kirkja*), 'chest' becomes *kist* (ON *kista*) and the Old English name Cese-wic is transformed into Keswick

l is often so light it disappears! In parts of Cumbria, 'wall' becomes *waw*, 'pole' is *pow*, and 'wool' is metamorphosed into *woo'*

r is a very distinctive sound — unique amongst the English counties. Unlike the rolled Scottish 'r', in the Cumbrian 'r' the tongue touches the roof of the mouth just once, producing a 'flapped' 'r' sound as in *threes* ('trees')

The Glottal Stop

Like the grey squirrel, the infamous glottal stop, rather like a short cough, seems to be invading from the south. It is endemic in Barrow, where 'pretty' is *pri'y* and hospital is *'ospi'al*, and there is some evidence to suggest that it has spread to Whitehaven and Work-ington, but throughout most rural areas it is not conspicuous.

Abbreviations & Symbols

abbr	abbreviation
c	circa
cf	compare with
I	Icelandic
D	Danish
N	Norwegian
OE	Old English (the language of the Anglo-Saxons)
OF	Old French (Norman French)
ON	Old Norse (the language of the Vikings)
pron	pronounced
S	Swedish
ð	used in Icelandic to simulate a soft 'th' sound
qv	which see

A

Aakseyd Hawkshead
abacka behind, at the back of
abackerbeyont at a great distance away
abide to put up with, tolerate *Ah can't abide it!* (cf *bide*)
acos for the reason, because
accouchers male midwives (cf *howdy*) (see *groaning cheese*)
across met with *Ah cum across an auld nebbur i' Peerith* (qv)
addle to earn (I *öðlast*, to acquire) *'Addling brass'* is earning money *Is tha addling owt much?* (cf *eddle, yaddle*)
addled bad, rotten, especially eggs; also a euphemism for intoxicated (cf *in liquor, fluz'd, kalied, kettelt, tight*)
aforehand done before
aforetime previously; the old days *They'd had some bother aforetime about t' tups* (qv) *and t' dykes* (qv)
afore, afront before *git thi clogs off afore tha cums in* (OE *onforan*, before)
ahint behind (OE *aet-hindan*, behind)
aiblins possibly *Willsta* (qv) *come a' Mundy? Aiblins ah may*
akin related, of the same race (I *kyn*, race)

alag leaning; on one side
alanga on account of, for sake of *It's o' alanga thee*
ald, auld old (see *auld wives' hake*)
ale posset (see *posset*)
alegar malt vinegar, from sour ale, as vinegar is from sour wine (cf *elliker*)
alley boy's marble, possibly because early marbles were made from alabaster (see *taws¹*)
all-owerish a feeling of weakness or listlessness *Ah nobbut* (qv) *feel a bit all-owerish ta-day*
allus always
Ambleside Bridge House one of the most photographed buildings in the Lake District. The one-up, one-down house over Stock Gill was probably a summer house of the Braithwaite family of Ambleside Hall. In the 1840s the house was the home of the Rigg family who brought up six children there, and early this century a local cobbler used the lower floor as his premises, the upper storey being a pigeon loft. In 1926 it was bought by local subscription and given to the National Trust. The

Bridge House, Ambleside.

story — still told by coach drivers — that it was the home of a Scotsman who wished to avoid paying ground rent is regrettable and apocryphal.

Amelsed Ambleside. Curiously, in 1274 the place-name was spelt 'Amelset'.

anaw, an' all as well, also, into the bargain. Often used for emphasis *He git a clip't lug* (qv), *he did an' all!*

Anchorites lay hermits who undertook the care of the poor and needy. John Speed's map of Kendal (1610) clearly marks 'The Ankeriche'; the site is occupied by Anchorite House, built in 1771, and now surrounded by the Kirkbarrow housing estate. Folklore says that a knight, having lost the affections of the fair Lady

Blanche, joined a crusade and learned the arts of eastern medicine. On his return, he built a beehive hut by Kirkbarrow Well, and used its waters to perform miraculous cures of leprosy and other diseases. A good story — but sadly lacking any foundation.

aneath below *T' price o' haver's* (qv) *a gay bit aneath what it yance* (qv) *was*

anenst opposite to; over against

anger inflammation (I *angr*, pain)

angert inflamed, red, glowing

angs awns, the beard of barley (Furness, South and West Cumbria)

a'ower, ahower indeed, at any rate, however

Appleby Horse Fair instituted by a Royal Charter of James ll. Held on the second Tuesday and

Washing horses in the River Eden during the Appleby Horse Fair.

Wednesday in June, it attracts gipsy families from all over the North of England. Sadly, it has gained a somewhat unfortunate reputation.

Apple-Noddy Day a Furness expression meaning April Fool's Day (see **gowk²**):

> *Apple-noddy's past an' gone*
> *An' thou's a noddy for*
>   *thinkin' on*   local rhyme

April-gowk (see **gowk**)

archery The archers of Cumbria have long been famous. The Kendal Bowmen, who wore a uniform of **Kendal green** (qv) and buff adorned with arrow buttons, acquitted themselves with distinction at the Battle of Flodden in 1513. It was obligatory for men to practise archery after the Sunday church service, and many Cumbrian church porches have arrow-sharpening marks where, waiting for their turn at the butts, the archers would hone their arrows. At Cartmel Fell Chapel there are not only arrow-sharpening marks on the church porch but also on several of the rock outcrops on the nearby fellside. By the nineteenth century, archery had become a sport, and at Whitehaven the Company of Archers competed for a medal designed for them by the famous architect, Sir Robert Smirke. (see also **yew trees**)

argify to debate or argue

ark large wooden chest to hold meal, oat bread etc (I *örk*, OE *aerc*, chest)

arles, earles money paid to farm servants on hiring as a token of their hiring; usually one shilling (cf *earnest money*, *festing penny*, *yerls*) (see **hiring fairs**)

armhole armpit (cf *oxter*) (Furness and Cartmel)

arr scar, scratch, mark (I *ör*, a scar)

arrals skin disease known as ring-worm, believed to be contracted by contact with cattle

arran web cobweb (OF *araigne*)

arsle a fidget

Arthur, King (see **King Arthur**)

arval, arvel refreshments given at a funeral, a funeral feast. *Arval bread* was a small bun, always made of the best wheat flour, which was given to each mourner at the graveside. This was taken home to be eaten in the mourner's house. In some areas, *arval cheese* and *arval ale* were also distributed in the same manner. (see **funeral biscuits**) (I *arfleifð*, inheritance)

as¹ that *he said as he wod*

as² who *them as can mun* (qv) *come*

aside on beside, near, by the side of *hard aside on*, close by

ask¹ newt, lizard; a *watter ask* is a water newt, and a *dry ask* is a lizard

The watter ask.

ask² cold, a sharp wind. In Furness *(h)ask* is dry, cold weather (I *hastur*, harsh)

aslew not square or straight *his cap's on aslew*

asscat one who habitually stays by the fire

assel axle; *assel-tree*, axle-tree of a cart

assel-teeth molars (I *jaxl*, molar)

asteead instead

'at¹ that *He sed 'at he was gaan til Amelsed* (qv)

'at² to, in, about *Ah can do nowt* (qv) *mair at it!*

'at's that is, that are, which are *Them 'at's here, speak out*

atter spider (I *eitur*, OE *atter*, poison)

attercob, attercop spider's web

attermite Westmorland term meaning a family likeness, a chip off the old block (I *aettarmot*, family likeness)

atterpile Cartmel term for a small, stinging fish

atween between *Sit atween us*

atween whiles in the meantime

auld Nick Devil (cf *donnat*)

Auld Wives' Hake yearly gathering or convivial meeting, usually at Christmas. Young and old of both sexes attended, and the evening was spent in tea-drinking, card-playing and dancing.

> *We drank five cups o' tea*
> *apiece*
> *At hauf a pund o' cake;*
> *An' then we hed a jig er twa*
> *To finish off the Hake*
>   old rhyme

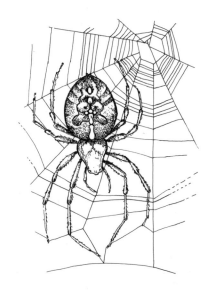

An atter and an attercob.

averish greedy, hungry, eating in a *giversum* (qv) manner

away to go away as in *'Ah'll away to bed'*

awsom appalling, awful

ax, ass to ask (west, south and far north-east of Cumbria) (OE *acsian*, to ask)

ax't oot the wedding banns being published three times

aye always, ever. In the Icelandic Landnamabok the burial mound of Torf-Einarr is described as *ae graenn*, ever green. *Aye* is also commonly used as an alternative for 'yes'. In South Cumbria, *aye, aye* is regarded as a friendly greeting. (I *ae*, ever, always)

ayont beyond

B

babblement silly discourse, foolish chatter

back can a metal can carried on the back for transporting milk

back end autumn *'T' back end's alus t' bare-end'* is a local proverb

back hander a blow with the knuckles *He giv him a reet back hander!*

back heel a Cumberland and Westmorland **wrestling** (qv) move

backset an' forset beset on all sides; surrounded by difficulties

back up to be angry *He's got 'is back up*

back-word cancellation of a booking *He's given back-word*

bacon stave slice of bacon tied around the neck with a woollen cloth as a cure for a sore throat (see **folk cures**)

bad difficult; **Bad at beat** means difficult to overcome

baddest worst *Aye, it's t' baddest thing 'at* (qv) *could hev happen't*

badger to brow-beat, to intimidate

badly sick, unwell *he looks reet badly*

bad man's posy purple dead-nettle (Carlisle area)

bad word verbal abuse *he got t' bad word fra t' gaffer* (qv)

baggings (see *bait*)

bags, bagsy childrens' term for claiming a place in a game, eg *bags me ferry* (qv) (see also *laggy*)

bain near (I *beinn*, straight, short). In Cumberland and Furness, *bain-est way* means the shortest way (I *beinstr vegr*, the shortest route).

bairn (see *barn*)

bait food for the mid-morning break which was usually taken to the place of work in a *bait box* (cf *baggings, drinkin'*)

bakst'n a flat stone, usually slate[1] (qv), underneath which a fire was lit. Large quantities of *haver bread* (qv) were then baked. Smaller quantities were made on an iron *girdle* (qv).

ball money sum of money given by wedding parties at church gates to children, traditionally to buy balls, though in the west of the county it was used to buy sweets

bang to strike, beat, surpass (I *bang*, hammering)

bank barn barn built on a hillside. Cattle are housed in the lower floor, but fodder is stored in the floor above them, the entrance being via a ramp or bank on the upper slope. The term was coined in 1963 by Professor R W Brunskill. (see *coo-as*)

bank up to collect together *bank up t' fire*

bannock cake of oatmeal and treacle, seasoned with ginger; *bannock-feaast* meant having a flat face and a snub nose

banty bantam; often used to describe a man who was 'vertically challenged'

bar except *It's aw ower bar t' shoutin'*

bargest a frightening spirit which has the power of foretelling death

bark troublesome cough

bark at t' heck (qv) to wait outside the door

bark'd bruised *Ah's bark'd my shins*

The bargest had the power of foretelling death and calamity.

barley sugar thin stick of clear toffee, traditionally twisted into a spiral

barn child (*bairn* in north Cumbria) (I, N, D, S *barn*, child)

barns' barns grandchildren

Barra Barrow-in-Furness — not to be confused with the island in the Outer Hebrides. And 'Furness' is pronounced *Furness*, not Fur*ness* as the computerised lady announcer on Lancaster rail station seems to think ...

barring out The annual schoolboy riot of *barring out* the schoolmaster from his school would today be termed a 'sit-in'. The object seems to have been to persuade the master to grant longer holidays. Most *barring outs* seem to have been amicable affairs, and doting parents such as Sir Daniel Fleming of Rydal regularly rewarded their sons with small monetary sums. The following rhyme was often chanted:

Bar him oot, bar him oot
Bar him oot wi' a pin;
Gie's a month's helida'
Er we'll nivver let ye in

At Mallerstang School the pupils reminded the master that the Brough Hill Fair extended over two days with the rhyme:

Two days at Brough Hill
  we hope you'll remember
That the first of October
  and the last of September

Barrow, Sir John (1764–1848) Born at Dragley Beck, Ulverston, the young John Barrow worked as an accounts clerk in a Liverpool iron foundry, then as a teacher of mathematics at Greenwich. In 1792 he was invited to join Lord McCartney's embassy to China and his subsequent book, *Travels in China*, proved very popular. Later, as McCartney's private secretary, he visited Cape Colony. Having attracted William Pitt's attention, he was appointed Second Secretary to the Admiralty, a post he occupied until 1845, apart from a short break in 1806. Although not an Arctic explorer himself, Barrow dreamed of opening up the North West Passage to India and he actively encouraged Ross, Parry and Franklin to that end. The northernmost point of the American continent, named Point Barrow, is a fitting memorial, but he also was one of the founder members of that important catalyst to nineteenth century exploration, the Royal Geographical Society. Two years after his death, a facsimile of Smeaton's Eddystone lighthouse was erected on a hill overlooking his birthplace. His book *The Mutiny of the Bounty* told the story of another

Cumbrian — Fletcher Christian (qv).

Bassenthat Bassenthwaite

batter drystone wall (qv) which decreases in thickness upwards is said to *batter*

battlin' stean stone on which coarse hemp *sarks* (qv) were beaten on wash day in order to soften them

battlin' stick, beetlin' stick wooden stick or paddle used to beat clothes on wash days

bawtry elder tree (cf *bortree*)

Baynes, Mary, of Tebay enjoyed a certain notoriety as an early nineteenth century witch, with an ability to cast evil spells on her neighbours and to make strange prophecies. One such was that horseless fiery carriages would one day hurtle at great speed along the Lune Valley. Within a generation of her death, engineers built the railway line through Tebay which carried those fiery engines at exactly the spot Mary had indicated ... (see **witchcraft**)

beal, beel the lowing of cattle; the sound of crying; to bawl *Ah'll gi'*

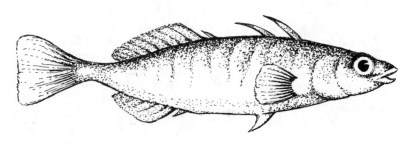

A beany-prick.

tha something to beal about! (I *baula*, the lowing of cattle)

bealen howling
Ya dismal, dark December neet,
When t' wind in t' chimley sood,
Com bealen doon off Cross Fell heets
A helm (qv) *rough and loud*
                                            Whitehead

beany-prick stickleback (Furness)

bearded wall has a thick layer of earth on the top in which quickthorns are planted. An item in the Morland Church accounts refers to '... bearding the kirkgarth wo' '

bearings bundles of rushes carried in procession during a *rushbearing* (qv); also known as *burdens*

bearmouth horizontal adits from which coal was mined without the use of a shaft

bears crude matting made from the peelings from rushes when *rushlights* (qv) were made

beas, beece, bees, beast cows or cattle generally

beast milk, beastings milk of a newly-calved cow, used for custards and puddings (cf *bull-jumpings*)

beaste to thrash with a stick or a cudgel

beck stream; common throughout Cumbria except in those areas bordering Scotland when the term becomes *burn* (ON *bekkr*, a stream)

beck-bibby water ouzel

bed-fast confined to bed by illness *Ah've been that badly* (qv), *I've been bed-fast for nigh on* (qv) *three weeks* (cf *laid up*)

bee boles square recesses in **drystone walls** (qv), intended to hold the straw bee *skeps* which they sheltered from the cold north wind. *Bee boles* generally face south to make maximum use of the sun.

bee bread brown substance in honeycomb

beece, bees (see *beas*)

bee coat cover of straw or fern placed over the bee hive

beeld (see *bield*)

beet to stoke or feed a fire (I *baeta*, to improve, mend, repair)

beetlin' stick (see *battlin' stick*)

beetin stick stick used for firing under a *girdle plate* (qv) when baking *haver bread* (qv)

Belfield, Rasselas a freed slave, a native of Abyssinia, who died on 16th January, 1822, aged thirty-two years, and is buried at the east end of Bowness churchyard. The inscription on his gravestone is poignant:

A slave by birth I left my
*   native Land*
And found my Freedom on
Britanias [sic] *Strand*
Blest Isle! Thou Glory of the
*   Wise and Free!*
Thy Touch alone unbinds the
Chains of Slavery

bellman official who made public announcements ringing a bell and 'calling'. In February 1812, the diarist William Fleming recorded that the bellman of Ulverston was incapacitated and therefore he employed one William Sandys to deputise for him and 'call' a shawl which had been found by the

watchman. Sandys carried out his
duties in dialect rhyme:

There was found in the street
By the watchman last neet,
A shawl, very wet wi' t' rain
When I'm paid for t' calling
I'll give over bawling
And the owner may have it
again

The bellman — a popular figure in
several Cumbrian towns.

Bellmen at Carlisle, Kendal, Dalton and Ulverston still maintain
the tradition.

bellying swelling in a **drystone
wall** (qv) just before it *rushes* (qv)

Beltane fires bonfires lit on

prominent hills on the eve of May
Day. Clearly these fires were a relic
of pagan fire-worship, and it was
advisable to carry a branch of
rowan (qv) when visiting the fire
to ward off the *evil eye* (qv)

bensal to thrash repeatedly and
severely

berrier old name for a thresher
berryin' bigg — to thresh barley
with a *flail* (qv) (I *berja,* to strike,
hit, beat, thrash)

berries gooseberries (see *grossers,
goosegogs*)

besom broom, usually made of
birch twigs or heather. In Cumbrian folklore the *besom* was a
potent symbol of fertility, and this
is reflected in the custom in which
married women jumped over a
besom; those who were not successful in this exercise were pronounced *the next for the straw.*
(see *groaning cheese, living over
the brush*) (OE *besema,* broom)

bessy, bessy blakelin yellowhammer

bessy blackcap black-headed
bunting

Bessy Brownbags (see *pace egg
song*)

betimes occasionally *betimes
he's queer as Dick's hat band* (qv)

better[1] recovered from an illness
Ah's quite better now

better[2] improve *he can't better
hissel* means he cannot improve
his present position

Betty Yewdale well-known dialect story by A C Gibson in which
the author presents a very different
and less romantic portrait of Betty
and her husband Jonathan to that

given by Wordsworth in *The Excursion*

bever to tremble

Bewcastle Cross This stands in St Cuthbert's churchyard, and is surrounded by some of the wildest, cloud-catching fells in England. Described by R G Collingwood as 'perhaps the first extant masterpiece of Early English stone carving', it dates from c AD 675. Covered with the vine-scrolls, birds and

Leaping over a besom was the traditional method of telling which wife was 'the next for the straw'.

11

geometric patterns so character-istic of the Anglian craftsmen who carved it, this cross is not merely a remarkable artistic achievement, it also boasts the oldest known sundial in Britain on its south face.

The seventh century Bewcastle Cross has the earliest example of a sundial in the country.

Rather than indicating our system of hours, it illustrates the Anglo-Saxon system of 'tides', still re-membered in such words as 'noon-tide' and 'eventide'. (see **mass dials**)

bezzel   to beat severely

bid   to invite to a gathering, usually a funeral or a wedding (cf *warn*) (I *bjoða*, to invite, OE *biddan*, to ask)

bidden funerals A *funeral bidder* was appointed to visit each family in a dale to announce the name of the deceased and *bid* representatives to attend the funeral. If *bidden*, every effort was made to attend the interment, since failure to do so would be regarded as a gross insult to the family and the deceased. In Sedbergh, announcements of deaths and funeral arrangements are still displayed in shop win-dows. (see *bidding-round*, *laiting*, *warn*)

bidden weddings Neighbours and friends were often *bidden* or invited to attend the wedding, and sometimes a *public wedding* was advertised by means of printed handbills. This involved an open invitation to anyone to attend the festivities — but at a certain point in the celebration, the bride would sit with a pewter plate on her knees and guests were expected to make a monetary contribution to the future happiness of the couple. At Keswick, early in the nineteenth century, some £70 was donated at the wedding of Henry Stoddart, and at Holm Cultram £100 was given to another couple. **Public weddings** usually included such entertainments as foot and horse races, as well as leaping and **wrestling** (qv) competitions. (see *bridecakes*, **throwing the stocking**, *sneckin' up t' yat*)

bidding-round area fixed by custom within which it was traditional to *bid* (qv) neighbours to a funeral or wedding (cf *laiting*)

bide to endure, to put up with *Ah can't bide it* (cf *abide*)

bield, beeld place of shelter; a fox den (I *baeli*, a den)

bigg six rowed barley (I *bygg*, N *bygg*, D *byg*)

biggin a building (I *bygging*)

bink narrow ledge of rock; narrow shelf

bink't *crag-fast* (qv), applied to fell sheep

birk birch tree, Coleridge's 'Lady of the Woods'. Despite its delicate appearance, it is the hardiest of our native trees and is found at an altitude of 2,000 feet (600m) above sea level. (ON *björk*, OE *beorc*, birch tree)

Bishop of Barf The legend says that a bishop once stayed at the Swan Inn, Thornthwaite. After indulging over-freely in liquor, he made a wager with his clerk to ride to the top of Lord's Seat — but sadly merely reached a point known as Bishop's Rock on Barf, where he fell from his horse and was killed. The landlord of the Swan arranges for the rock to be whitewashed regularly in memory of his ecclesiastical guest.

bity tongue pepperwort plant

blaan oot, blown out disqualified in a contest or competition. The expression is still heard at **Grasmere Sports** (qv) when a registered competitor fails to appear.

blackin' scolding; verbal abuse '... I set on an' geh them o' sike a blackin' as they willn't seeun forgit' *Betty Yewdale* (qv), A C Gibson

blackberries blackcurrants

Black Boar of Stricklandgate sign of the brushmakers outside Black Hall, a former brush works in Stricklandgate, Kendal. This is a facsimile, the original being in the Museum of Lakeland Life and Industry at Abbot Hall. Observant viewers will see that the animal appears to be female ...

Black Dub obelisk at the source of the River Lyvennet, which commemorates the occasion on the 8th August 1651, when King Charles II rallied his troops on the march from Scotland to the disastrous Battle of Worcester. The monument was carved in 1843 by Thomas Bland of Regill.

black hole common expression for the local gaol or lock-up

blackjack coalfish (Whitehaven); at Ravenglass and Maryport the same fish is known as *bluffin*

black kites, brummel kites blackberries (bramble berries). Regional variations include *blackbums* (Low Furness), *bumbly kites* (Great Langdale) and *bummel kites* (northern Cumbria).

black lead (see *wad*)

black peats (see *peat pot*)

The Black Boar of Stricklandgate, Kendal.

black powder gunpowder (cf *jack*)

Blamire, Susanna (1747–1794) born near Dalston, Susanna Blamire is well known for her Scottish lyrics and Cumbrian dialect poems. She is commemorated by a tablet unveiled in Carlisle Cathedral in 1994.

blanchard, blenkard one-eyed fighting cock, a veteran of many *cock mains* (qv)

blate shy *A blaat cat meks a prood* [bozld] *moose*

blather, blether foolish, noisy talk

blatherskite, bletherskite a gossip, a garrulous person (cf *clash*)

blatin' crying, bawling *Gi ower blatin', thoo girt taggelt* (qv) *!*

Blawith Church Bell In 1781 the vestry-men and inhabitants of the parish of Blawith, south of Coniston, decided that a steeple and a bell should be added to their church. Unfortunately, finances were rather meagre so a portion of the parish was auctioned to raise the necessary funds, occasioning the rhyme:

> *Blawith poor people*
> *An auld church and a new*
> *   steeple,*

As poor as Hell
They had to sell
A bit of fell
To buy a bell
Blawith poor people

blea   blue, hence Blea Tarn and *blea berries* (whortle berries) (I *blár*, blue)

bleb   blister; vessicle on seaweed; in Cartmel the word is used for small, white jellyfish which do not sting

blenkard   (see *blanchard*)

blinders   (see *gloppers*)

blobbing   to fish for crabs using fish-heads (Workington)

Susanna Blamire, an eighteenth century dialect poet.

blood alley   glass marble streaked with red (see *alley, taws¹*)

bloodstick   (see *fleam*)

bloomery hearths   crude, iron-smelting hearths, usually in a location where local charcoal could be readily obtained and where haematite iron ore could be brought by water — eg a lakeshore. There are many examples around the shores of Coniston Water.

bluebill   widgeon (cf *scaup*) (Cartmel)

blue milk   skimmed milk (see **cheese**)

bluffin   (see *blackjack*)

Bob Yak Day   Royal Oak Day, the 29th May. Probably originally *Yak Brobb* (qv) *Day*:

Royal Oak Day
The 29th of May,
If you don't give us a holiday
We'll all run away
                children's rhyme

bobbers   boy's marble too big to shoot with — it had to be bowled or pitched (Furness); in west Cumbria *dobbers* was used (see *taws¹*)

bobbing the apple   often played on Hallowe'en. A horizontal pole was suspended from a beam; at one end was hung an apple on a string, while at the other end was a lighted candle. The competitors had to take a bite out of the apple without causing the candle to be extinguished. (see **Duck Apple Night**)

bodderment   perplexity, anxiety. *Bobby Banks' Bodderment* is a well-known dialect story by A C Gibson.

boddersom troublesome

bog-trotters those who lived on the mosses of the Anglo-Scottish border, who were obliged to use a gentle trot rather than a heavy tread which would result in immersion in the bog

bogey, bogie home-made go-cart with four pram wheels; the front wheels can be steered by means of a rope

A bogey.

boggart ghost, apparition (? Celtic *bwg*, ghost)

boggle (see *bargest, boggart*)

bone setters local amateur osteopaths, much called upon to set both human and animal bones. Some possessed a surprising degree of anatomical knowledge

and many used the powdered roots of comfrey or *knit-bone* as a form of plaster.

bonny pretty, of good appearance

boolies children's hoops, usually made of iron, but wooden *boolies* were also a traditional Christmas decoration. Before Christmas trees became popular in the mid-nineteenth century, two wooden hoops, often from the outside of fruit barrels, were fitted together to form a crude globe. This was then decorated with those pagan symbols of Yuletide, holly and ivy, and sugar apples. In some parts of Cumbria they were known as *kissing bushes* (qv).

boon ploughing the ploughing of land done gratuitously by neighbours for a new, incoming tenant. Reporting a boon ploughing in Furness in 1815, the diarist William Fleming recorded that the new farmer, Jon Darley, promised his helpers 'a dinner, and plenty of ale, spirits and tobacco ... which has more attraction and inducement than the most extravagant wages he could have offered'. (see *clay daubin, merry neet, timber raising*)

boose, bouse, booas stall for a cow (I *bás*, stall)

borran rough, craggy places with large boulders often used by foxes as a refuge (see also *fox screws, fox traps*)

Borrowdale gowks an oft-told tale which relates how the good people of Borrowdale wished to retain spring all year round so they built a wall to keep in the cuckoo or **gowk** (qv) — from whence they earned the name **Borrowdale gowks**. The plot failed, and one dalesman was heard to shout as the bird flew away: *'Nay, if we'd nobbut* (qv) *laid anudder line o' cams* (qv), *we'd o' copped 'im ...'*

Borrowdale sop white cloud which often gathers over Sty Head and Sprinkling Tarn. If it moves away in the direction of Great Langdale, rain may be expected; if it passes to the east of Borrowdale, fine weather will continue.

borrowed days a number of unexpectedly fine days in early spring or autumn

bortree elder tree; a *bortree stick* was often carried in the pocket as a charm against **witchcraft** (qv) (cf *bawtry*)

bortree wine, bortree Joan elderberry wine

bottom winds fierce winds which suddenly blow down a fellside, often disturbing one part of a lake while leaving another section perfectly calm. They are especially noticeable on Derwentwater and Bassenthwaite Lake.

'Bound Devil' carved into a slab of stone in St Stephen's Church, Kirkby Stephen. Discovered in 1870, it appears to represent a horned and bearded figure, bound hand and foot. Local folklore suggests that this is Satan, but it is more likely to represent the pagan Norse god Loki who, for his involvement in the death of Balder, was bound and thrown

The 'Bound Devil' of Kirkby Stephen is probably the Norse god Loki.

into a snake pit. (see **Gosforth Cross**)

Bowder Stone huge *bowder* or boulder which was left perched on its keel by the retreating Borrowdale glacier some 10,000 years ago. In the nineteenth century it became one of the major tourist attractions, delighting and astounding the early **Lakers** (qv). **Joseph Pocklington** (qv), that irrepressible self-publicist, built a cottage nearby, and installed an old woman whose job was to 'show' the tourists the Bowder Stone! He arranged for a hole to be cut in the base so that the visitors could, in the words of Southey, 'gratify themselves by shaking hands with the old woman' underneath the stone.

Bowness-on-Solway's bells supposed to have been stolen by a party of Scottish raiders. On being hotly pursued, the Scots abandoned the bells in the middle of the *wath* (qv) across the Solway, from where, it is said, the ghostly sound of bells can be heard on still evenings. What is certain is that there are two bells in Bowness Church, both filched from Scotland in revenge — one from Dornock and one from Middlebie. Until recently, whenever a new vicar of Bowness was inducted, the minister of Dornock would make a formal request for the return of the bells to Scotland; the vicar's reply was always the same — 'when ours come back from the sea'.

Bowscale Tarn This cold, north-facing tarn in Mosedale has two legends associated with it. One concerns two immortal fish which supposedly live there. Wordsworth's *Song at the Feast of Brougham Castle* mentions:

'... the undying fish that swim
Through Bowscale-tarn ...'

but in 1703 Bishop Nicolson had insisted that the tarn was 'so cold, yt nothing lives in it. Fish have been put in: But they presently dy.'

The tarn is also reputed to reflect the stars at noon, but Harriet Martineau, ever the realist, adds 'but under so many conditions, that it will be a wonder if any body has the luck to see them'.

bracken clock ladybird

braken dales plots of land growing bracken which were allocated to farmers. The bracken was cut and used for bedding for animals.

bracken sleds heavy wooden sleds used for transporting bracken down steep fellsides; wheeled vehicles would overturn on these steep slopes, but *bracken sleds* remained stable.

braffin horse collar (see *gurn*)

Bragg, Melvyn the best-known contemporary. Cumbrian writer. His Cumbrian trilogy (*The Hired Man, A Place in England, Kingdom Come*) shows a deep and affectionate understanding of the people, places, dialect and traditions of Cumbria, while *The Maid of Buttermere* ranks as one of the finest British historical novels. *A Christmas Child* is a sensitive re-telling of the Christmas story set in his birthplace, Wigton, and *Credo* is concerned with the legend of *St Bega* (qv).

brake (see *dressing brake*)

brandreth iron tripod placed over a hearth fire for cooking purposes (cf *trivet*) (I brandreið, a grate)

brant steep; except in the northern part of the county where 'steep' is more common (I brattur, steep)

brass money, as in *it'll cost a gay* (qv) *bit o' brass*; but it can

Bracken sleds were once common on Cumbrian hill-farms.

also mean impudence or assurance, as in **he's plenty of brass in his face**

brass'd off disillusioned, disappointed

brat pinafore or coarse apron. On Stockdale Moor, near Gosforth, there are many prehistoric stone cairns known collectively as **Samson's Bratful**. The legend says that

A brandreth.

Satan (later altered to Samson) was carrying stones in his **brat** when the strings broke and let the stones fall onto the fellside.

bray to chastise and bruise someone

bread and cheese leaves of the hawthorn (qv), eaten by children in the spring

bread and scrape slice of bread spread with fat — usually dripping — which is then scrapped off again to conserve as much as possible. A euphemism for a very poor sort of diet — *Aye, they nobbut lived on bread an' scrape.* (see **taties-an'-point**)

bread cupboards carved oak cupboards forming part of the partition wall which divided the *fire house* (qv) from the bower or best bedroom and the pantry or larder on the ground floor of seventeenth century farmhouses. Many are dated and bear the initials of the farmer and his wife.

They were often used for the storage of unleaven *haver bread* (qv). Sometimes referred to as *court cupboards*.

breast plough   (see *push plough*)

bree   bustle, hurry

bridecake   thin currant cake served at weddings. At a certain point in the celebrations, the bride sat on a wooden chair with her head covered with a cloth; the bridegroom then broke the *bridecake* over her head and the pieces were distributed among the guests. One authority suggests that the more pieces the cake fell into, the more children the couple would have. (see *bidden wedding*, throwing the stocking, *sneckin' up t' yat*)

bridewain   originally the *kist* (qv) or chest in which the bride conveyed her belongings to her new house, but by the mid-eighteenth century it came to refer to the collection made for the newlyweds at the wedding feast (see *bidden wedding*)

brig   bridge (ON *bryggja*)

Bridge House   (see Ambleside Bridge House)

Broad Stand   Between Scafell and Scafell Pike, the highest land in England, lies a 30 foot (9m) rockface known as Broad Stand. This, according to folk legend, was the site of the first rock climb/ descent in the country. It was accomplished by no less a person than Samuel Taylor Coleridge in August 1802. He had climbed Scafell and, seeing Scafell Pike in the distance, decided to climb that too, but this necessitated descending

Broad Stand. He began to drop down a series of small crags without much difficulty:

... but the Stretching of the
muscle of my hands and arms,
and the jolt of the Fall on my Feet,
put my whole limbs in a Tremble,
and I paused, and looking down,
saw that I had little else to
encounter but a succession of
these little Precipices — it was, in
truth a Path that in very hard
Rain is, no doubt, the channel of
a most splendid Waterfall. So I
began to suspect that I ought not
to go on; but then unfortunately,
though I could with ease drop
down a smooth rock of 7 feet
high, I could not climb it, so go on
I must; and on I went

Broad Stand is today classified as a rock climb.

brobbs, brogs   bough or a branch of a tree. *Brobbing the sands* is a term used for the marking of a route, using branches, across the sands of Morecambe Bay (see **Cross Sands Route**). Also used for the straw in the hat of a person wishing to be taken on at a *hiring fair* (qv).

brocken   broken

brocken mooth'd   sheep which has lost some of its teeth

Brocken spectre   optical phenomenon first observed on the Brocken Mountain in Germany. Occasionally seen in the Lake District by walkers on mountain summits when the sun is behind them, casting huge shadows onto mist-filled valleys below. The observers can sometimes see halos

*A bridecake was broken over the bride's head
as part of the wedding celebrations.*

'Brobbing the sands' of Morecambe Bay with small branches to mark a safe route.

or 'glories' around each figure, ranging from violet on the inside through blue, green and yellow to red on the outside. (see also *Souther Fell phantom army*)

Brocklebank, Captain Daniel Born in Torpenhow, the son of a local curate, Daniel Brocklebank (1742–1801) became the best-known of Whitehaven's eighteenth century shipbuilders and the founder of the oldest shipping line in the country. The firm later moved to Liverpool, where T and J Brocklebank amalgamated with the Cunard Line.

brod mark made by the tide on a beach where it leaves whatever flotsam is washed up (Cartmel)

brogs (see *brobbs*)

brossen burst, cracked *'Why don't you ring the other bell?' "Cos it's brossen, Mr Bishop'*

brossenful fit to burst after eating too much

Brough Holly Night riotous custom, now no longer respected, in which a holly bush was illuminated with candles and *rushlights* (qv) and carried through the town on Twelfth Night. At a given signal, the bush was thrown into the assembled crowd, where gangs of youths fought to carry it off to rival inns.

Brough Stone strange stone on which several academic reputations have foundered. Unearthed in Brough Church in 1879, it was first thought to have a runic inscription commemorating an early Christian martyr. However, in 1884 it was proved to consist of five Greek hexameters reading:

Hermes of Commagene here,
Young Hermes in his sixteenth year
Entombed by fate, before his day
Beholding let the traveller say:
'Fair youth, my greetings to thy
shrine,
Though but a mortal course
be thine
Since all to soon thou wing'st
thy flight
From realms of speech to realms
of night
Yet no misnomer art thou shown
Who with thy namesake god art
flown'

Commagene is in modern Syria. Was Hermes the son of one of the many Greeks who accompanied the Roman army, especially as physicians? The original stone is in the Fitzwilliam Museum, Cambridge

brown leemers brown nuts ripe enough to drop from the husks (see *leem*)

brucellosis disease resulting in contagious abortion of calves. It was believed that the burial of a calf at the foot of the *byre* (qv) door would prevent the spread of the infection, and this was done in West Cumbria even as late as 1876. An alternative was to allow a goat in the *byre* with the cows.

Bruff Burgh-by-Sands

brummel kites (see *black kites*)

brush tail of a fox

buckie whelk (probably from the same root as the Manx gaelic *buckee*)

A buckie.

budge move, stir *budge up t' sconce* (qv) *then*

bullases, bullaces small, round plums

bull baiting Banned in 1835 along with **cockfighting** (qv), this barbarous activity was once popular in such towns as Kirkby Stephen, Keswick, Appleby, Wigton, Penrith and Kendal, where it was made illegal in 1790. It was believed that meat from a *baited* animal was more tender than that from a beast slaughtered normally, and therefore it was much sought after.

A bull head.

bull head tadpole or small fish

bull loup (see *montikitty*)

bull-jumpings milk from a cow immediately after calving which, when boiled, produces a custard-like substance (cf *beast milk*)

bull ring iron ring to which the bull was tethered for baiting (see *bull baiting*). To *shake the bull ring* was a challenge to a town or village to produce a champion to fight the shaker.

bull stang dragonfly (cf *horse stang*)

bum, bumbailey court bailiff who could sieze property in lieu of payment of fines (see also *flit*)

bumbly kites, bummel kites (see *black kites*)

burdens (see *bearings*)

Buroo twentieth century urban expression, mainly confined to Barrow, meaning the Employment Exchange — a Barrovian corruption of 'bureau' *He's bin to Buroo*'

butter leaves The leaves of the mountain dock, used for packing butter in the market basket.

butter sops like *rum butter* (qv) it was eaten at christenings and *wife days* (qv). That irrepressible early tourist, Joseph Budworth, witnessed its preparation in 1792:

... the [wheat] bread is cut into thin slices and placed in rows one above the other in a large kettle of 20 or 30 gallons ... butter and sugar are dissolved in a separate one, and then poured upon the bread, where it continues until it has boiled for some space and the bread is perfectly saturated with the mixture. It is then taken out and served up by way of a dessert

buzzer factory whistle or hooter. In certain areas of Barrow, the sound of either the shipyard buzzer or that of the steelworks was a weather portent — eg 'a rainy buzzer' Writing of Millom, Norman Nicholson acknowledged the same phenomenon in his poem *Weather Ear*.

byre (see *coo-as*)

C

Calgarth skulls The legend relates how Myles Philipson, who once owned Calgarth Hall on the shores of Windermere, coveted an estate owned by an elderly and respected couple, Dorothy and Kraster Cook. He falsely accused them of theft and had them executed. Afterwards their skulls appeared at Calgarth Hall and defied all efforts to get rid of them: they were buried, burned, reduced to ashes — but always they returned to haunt the Philipson family. Eventually, so the story goes, they were walled up, a solution which seemed to pacify the skulls, for soon after there were no more Philipsons left at Calgarth for them to frighten.

camerel, cameril, carmel curved piece of wood with notches at both ends on which a butcher hangs carcasses

camplin' cheek, sauce, contradiction *Ah'll hev none o' thi camplin, mind* (qv) *!*

cams serrated coping stones on top of a **drystone wall** (qv) (see also *footings, heartings, throughs*) (I *kambur,* a ledge of rock, a comb)

Candlemas, Cannelmas the 2nd February features regularly in weather lore:

*If the thrush sings afore
  Cannelmas Day
It does nowt after but repent
  and pray*

*If Cannelmas Day be
  sunshining and warm*

A camerel was used by butchers to suspend carcasses.

Tin 'cannel barks' not only protected candles and rushlights, they also prevented mice from enjoying a free meal.

Ye may mend yer oald mittens and look for a storm

If Cannelmas Day be fine and clear,
We'll get two winters in one year

candlesticks garden cowslips

cane-breaker small pieces of mica which, according to the folklore of children in the 1940s, would lessen the pain inflicted by the cane if rubbed on the hands. The author can testify that it didn't work!

cannel bark cylindrical tin box with a hinge and a hook on the back which was used to store candles and **rushlights** (qv). The box was positioned in a central location, and the hinged lid and tin construction prevented mice from eating the contents.

canny (see *conny*)

canny bit cautious term of comparison *Aye, ah feels a canny bit better*

cantin' coloquial Furness (mainly Barrow) expression for gossiping *She's a grand one fer cantin'* (cf *clattin'*) (*cant* is the Romany word for the language spoken by Gypsies

cap to top or surpass *'... canny auld Cummerland caps them aw still'* (Anderson). *It caps cut lugs* and *it caps hen-racing* both mean that it surpasses everything.

carding 'do'   social gathering for card playing. Games such as *three card lant*, *brag*, *nap* and whist were all popular. Often formed part of a *merry neet* (qv).

Carel   Carlisle

carlings   dried peas soaked overnight and fried in butter. They were traditionally eaten on Carling Sunday, the second Sunday before Easter. The Sundays in Lent were commemorated by the rhyme:

Tid, Mid, Misseray
Carling, Palm and Pace Egg Day

cat   (see *uggery welt*)

cat loup   in close proximity, nearby *it was within a cat loup*

catmallison   recess shelf or small carved cupboard, often above the *fire window* (qv), which contained the family Bible. Literally, a cupboard which the cat can't rob.

catterwauling   noisy nocturnal intrigues

caulkers, caakers, corkers   iron rims under **clog** (qv) soles, and at the toes and heels of shoes (cf *snoot bands*)

cawke   (see *wad*)

Cawthat   Calthwaite

chafts   jaws

chance barn   illegitimate child (see *merry-begatan*)

chang   noisy talk or clamour (Furness); also the cry of a pack of hounds

Chapel Sundays   Sundays in August and September at Bassenthwaite, Newlands, Thornthwaite and surrounding districts, when folk assemble from a distance, attend church service, dine with their friends and then adjourn to the inns to make merry in honour of the saint to whom the chapel was dedicated

char   Alpine trout found mainly but not exclusively in Windermere and Coniston lakes. The Rydal Hall papers contain many references to *char pies* and *potted char*; indeed, one writer has suggested that the seventeenth century Squire of Rydal, Sir Daniel Fleming, made the *char* 'an instrument of social diplomacy whereby he sweetened [or savoured] his intercourse with politicians and friends at court'. Many of these pies were enormous; in 1673 Sir Daniel despatched two *char pies* to the Earl of Carlisle which weighed 'near

A char dish.

twelve stone' (75kg)! In the nineteenth century, potted *char* remained popular, despite some evidence of over-fishing, and special earthenware dishes were produced, many having a picture of the fish incorporated into the design round the sides.

Charcoal Black and the Bonny Grey   a cock-fighting song, popular throughout Cumbria, the names and places being changed to suit several different locations

charms　(see **folk cures**)

chass　hurry　*Nae girt chass*

chats　small potatoes; small sticks used as fuel (Low Furness)

chatter hen, chitty　wren

chatter watter　tea. When tea became popular in the eighteenth century, it presented certain problems to dalesfolk; the story is told of a woman who received a pound of tea from her son in London — and promptly filled her clay pipe with it, declaring it to be superior to the best Virginia tobacco! Others saw the introduction of tea as a blow to the moral fibre of the area; the *Cumberland Pacquet* of October 1792 was particularly outspoken:

> *A correspondent says that in the neighbourhood of Greystoke, during the late harvest, added to an increase of wages, the female reapers had regularly their tea every afternoon, and the men toast and ale. How different is this from the beef-steak breakfasts of old! How degenerate is the present age and how debilitated may the next be!*

chatterment　small *flukes* (qv) (cf *spouse*) (Cartmel)

checks　knuckle bones used in a game

cheese　Although cheese was made for household consumption, Cumbria did not develop the reputation for cheese-making enjoyed by Wensleydale or Cheshire. Skim-milk or *blue-milk* (qv) cheese was commonly found on most Lakeland tables, but this was somewhat tough and was known as *wangy cheese* because, according to the story, *wangs* or leather shoelaces could be made from it! The Whillimoor area of West Cumberland was particularly famous for *Whillimoor wang*, a cheese which, when sold in Carlisle market, was described as being 'lank and lean but cheap and clean'.

chepster, cheppy　starling (cf *shep*)

chick nor child　The phrase *neither chick nor child* was often used to describe a couple who had no children or dependents (cf *kith ner kin*)

chig　to chew, often with with the front teeth　*it teks some chigin'*

chimla boke　(see *rannel baulk*)

chimley, chimla　chimney

chip　move in Cumberland and Westmorland **wrestling** (qv)

chitty　(see *chatter hen*)

choup　(see *shoup*)

Christian, Fletcher　(1764–1804?) The leader of the most notorious mutiny in English naval history was born at Moorland Close, two miles south of Cockermouth. After serving as a midshipman, Christian first sailed with Captain Bligh in 1786-7, and the two seem to have become good friends. During the ill-fated voyage of the *Bounty*, on which Christian was second-in-command, the friendship turned to hatred and rebellion, perhaps because Christian had succumbed to the charms of Tahiti and 'gone native'. Whatever were the reasons, the mutiny began on the 28th April 1789; Bligh and eighteen others were set adrift, and the *Bounty* sailed to Tahiti, then to Pitcairn Island, where the nine European men and Tahitian women founded the colony. In 1808 their descendants were discoved, but the fate of Fletcher Christian is unknown. Rumours that he returned to England and even met his former schoolfellow, William Wordsworth, in Bristol in 1795 are merely romantic speculation.

Christmas (see *Kersmas*)

Christmas goose the traditional Yuletide fare. Even in the early twentieth century, the goose grease was bottled and chests were rubbed with this to ward off colds and chills. Children were greased and then sewn into brown paper waistcoats which were not removed until spring. It didn't do much for their social life — but as a preventive embrocation it had no equal!

chuck to throw; *chuckin'-out time*, closing time for pubs

chunter, chunner to grumble in an undertone

cinder tea made by dropping a red-hot cinder into sweetened water. Used as a cure for a variety of stomach ailments and to bring up baby's wind. (see **folk cures**)

clack to chatter *'folks was gidderan i' kirk garth for a bit of a clack ...'* (*My Daily Round*, Rev W Clarke, (1804–1868))

clag, claggy sticky (D *kloeg*, sticky, loamy)

claggan treacle toffee

clam up satiated *Ah'm fair* (qv) *clam't up wi' poddish*

clap[1] to pat or fondle (I *klappa*, pat or stroke)

clap[2] to put or set, as in *Ah ne'er clap't eyes on him*

clap[3] patch of cow dung

clapbread unleaven *oatbread* which was the staple bread in the central fells, since wheat would seldom ripen in the short, damp growing season. The dough was *clapped* paper-thin on a wooden board before being slipped onto an iron *girdle* (qv) or a *bakst'n* (qv) and cooked until golden brown. (see **bread cupboards**, **haver bread**)

clapperclowe to beat and scratch; to strike two objects together to produce a strident noise

clart, clarty, clarted smeared with mud *Nay, tha's aw clarted up*

clash, clat scandal, gossip; sometimes used to describe a female gossip *She's a turble* [terrible] *clat* (cf *blatherskite*)

clashy rainy; stormy weather

clattin'[1] a blow to the ear with the fist

clattin'[2] (see *cantin'*)

clay daubin timber and clay house, usually in areas where building stone was not readily available — eg the Solway Plain. A newly-married couple would sometimes invite their friends and relatives to help them build their new house. The men would erect the wooden framework and dig the clay, the women carried chopped straw and small stones to mix with the clay, which was then laid in sheets on thin layers of straw to form the walls. A thatched roof of straw or heather completed the task, which could be finished in a day. (see **boon ploughing**, **timber raising**)

cleg　horsefly (I *kleggi*, horse fly)

A cleg.

clemmed　starved, parched. Dorothy Wordsworth uses the word in her *Journals*. (D *klemme*, to starve, I *klemma*, to pinch)

clever-clogs　a clever person; usually used in a satirical sense

Clifford, Lady Anne　Countess of Pembroke, 'Proud Northern Lady' — and 'Lady Bountiful' of Westmorland. Anne Clifford (1590 –1676) more or less rebuilt her Cumbrian castles at Pendragon, Brough, Appleby and Brougham; a formidable lady, she 'feared God and took her own part'. On one famous occasion she claimed a 'boon hen' as well as the manorial rent from a recalcitrant cloth

merchant. Eventually, forced by law to pay up in full, the merchant was invited to dinner by the good lady — and of course, the first dish was the hen! 'Come, Mr Murgatroyd', she said, 'let us be friends. Since your hen is served at my table, I will give you half.' Appropriately, Lady Anne is buried in St Lawrence's Church in Appleby, Westmorland's county town, where she had founded St Anne's Hospital, a group of almshouses for widows, in 1651.

Clifton　the last military battle on English soil was fought here in the fields just south of Penrith in December 1745. The Duke of Cumberland had hoped to capture Eamont Bridge and cut off the retreating Scots, but the Highlanders stood their ground. The outcome of the skirmish was inconclusive — both the Duke of Cumberland and Prince Charles Edward Stuart claimed victory.

clip¹　to shear sheep

clip²　a year's wool crop

clip³　to hit, strike　*Tha'll git a clip't lug* (qv)

clippin' time　sheep shearing. Unlike lambing, clipping was a time for celebration; the work was arduous but tobacco was provided, a special *clippin' drink* was brewed, tales were told and songs sung. And a *merry neet* (qv) always rounded off the *clippin'*! (see *hack pudding*)

1684 June twentieth Given to Reny, fidler [sic] for playing this day unto my clipper 6 pence

Rydal account books of Sir Daniel Fleming

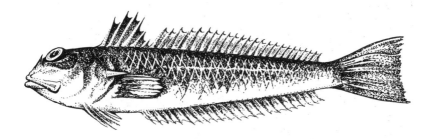

The clockermunjie has poisonous barbs on its dorsal fin.

clip't shortened *T' days is clip't in a bit at t' back end* (qv)

clock hen, clocker broody hen (OE *cloccian*, to cluck)

clockermunje strange word used along the Furness coasts for the weaver fish, which has poisonous barbs on the dorsal fin and the gills. Certainly to be avoided when *treading for fluke* (qv).

clockmaking Clockmaking in Cumbria was largely a family trade, often followed by several generations. Jonas Barber, senior, and Jonas Barber, junior, of Winster were the most famous exponents of the art in the seventeenth and eighteenth centuries, but other families such as the Philipsons followed the tradition. The Burton family worked in towns such as Kendal, Hawkshead and Whitehaven, the Haythornthwaites produced three generations of clockmakers, while the Pooley family established their reputation in Asby in the mid- and late eighteenth century. In Cockermouth, three women clockmakers, Mary Mitchell, Mary Metcalf (neé Mitch-ell) and Mary Simpson, produced some remarkably fine timepieces in the late eighteenth and early nineteenth centuries.

clog slate quarryman's term for a large piece of **slate**[1] (qv) blasted from the quarry face

clogs the most universal and practical footwear, worn by both dalesmen and women. The alder soles insulated the wearer from

Clogs were once worn by yeoman farmer and hired hand alike. The toe is protected by a brass 'snoot band'.

31

the damp and chill of the fields, and both the soles and the heels were protected from excessive wear by *caulkers* (qv) or iron rims. In the slate quarries, copper and lead mines, the workers lined their clogs with *wisps* (qv) or soft straw for warmth. (see *snoot bands*, *spring clogs*)

'clogs to clogs in three generations' mainly Lancashire expression, but used in Furness, reflecting the belief that poverty will return after the third generation

clog wheels primitive wooden wheels fixed to a wooden axle which turned underneath the cart, often producing an intolerable *jiking* (qv) sound. To minimize this, the cart driver would often carry with him an animal horn filled with grease which he would liberally *clart* (qv) on the *assel* (qv).

Primitive solid wooden clog wheels.

close clammy, moist weather

Close, 'Poet' (1816–1891) Cumbria's answer to William MacGonagall. A self-taught 'poet', who lived most of his life at Kirkby Stephen, John Close was a prolific writer of doggerel and 'metrical balderdash'. During the 1860s and 1870s he spent his summers on Bowness promenade selling his books of 'verse'. Those who offered even the slightest praise were eulogised in print, while those who criticised were severely castigated.

POET CLOSE AT HIS DESK.

Thanks to support from Lord Lonsdale, he was placed on the Civil List and awarded a pension of £50 — but this was removed after questions were asked in the Commons! 'Poet' Closes's *Ninth Christmas Book, 1878-79* contains this example of his skill:

With legs across, upon his chair,
And Lakes Books in his hand,
His anxious eyes cast everywhere,
In search of a demand,
From sultry noon to evening dews,
Sits Poet Close beneath the yews

Perhaps his epitaph was best stated by the *Dictionary of National Biography* which, with transparent honesty, declared that 'he had not a spark of literary talent of any kind'.

closehead quarry slate[1] (qv) quarry in which all the workings were underground

clot-head stupid individual

clot-iron crude 'bloom' iron smelted in a *bloomery hearths* (qv)

clout a cloth, hence *puddin'-clout, cheese clout*. Also:

Cast not a clout
Til May be out

which probably refers to May blossom rather than the month.

cluuts feet

cob to pull the hair as a punishment or penalty *he got a cobbin'*; also to kick the buttocks with the broadside of the foot

cobblement badly put together *nay, it's nowt but cobblement*

cobbles rounded stones worn smooth by the action of a river or the sea

cocker a cockfighter

cockfighting arguably the most popular Cumbrian sport until it was declared illegal in 1835. Drawing its support from a wide spectrum of society — from the local squire and clergymen to farm servants and village school lads — it was believed that *cocking* gave examples of gameness and pluck. Indeed, it might be said that the *cock pits* (qv) of Cumbria corresponded to the playing fields of Eton. The most popular season for cockfighting was Shrovetide,

when *cock mains* (qv) were held out of doors as well as indoors (*closed mains*) (see below, and *blanchard, Charcoal Black and the Bonny Grey, steg, Welsh mains*)

cocklemar oystercatcher (Cartmel) (cf *sea pie*)

A cocklemar, sea pie or sea pyat.

cock loaf a champion cock was a financial asset and much care went into their feeding. *Cock loaf* was a rich bread made from flour, eggs, milk, sugar and currants — with a secret ingredient which was usually sherry, rum or port wine. *Fed like a fighting cock* is still a common description of those individuals fed on gastronomic delicacies. (see **cockfighting**)

cock loft originally attics at the top of a farmhouse where fighting cocks were reared for the mains, but later used generally for any small attic room (see **cockfighting**)

cockly, cocklety unstable, unsteady *Yon* (qv) *coppy stool's* (qv) *cockly*

cock main contest in which several pairs of fighting cocks were matched against each other, thus twenty pairs were called called a *forty-cock main* (see **cockfighting**)

cock penny sums of money given to schoolboys, usually at Shrovetide. This money was given to the schoolmaster; some authorities argue that this supplemented his income, while others suggest that it allowed him to buy fighting cocks to pit against the birds brought to school by his pupils. What is certain is that 'penny' was a misnomer, for in 1675 Sir Daniel Fleming sent to his sons in Kendal '... to my son William 10 shillings, [to] Henry — being a captain — a broad 20 shilling piece in gold, and [to] Daniel 5 shillings for cockpennys to the master'. (see **cockfighting**)

cock pit circular fighting platform, about seventeen feet (5m) in diameter, surrounded by a ditch and an embankment. Spectators stood on the bank but only the *feeders* and the *setters*, who held the birds before the fight, were allowed beyond the ditch. One of the best examples in Cumbria is on the village green at Stainton in Furness, but another example may be seen in the traditional location — between the church and the school — at Heversham. At Penrith the cock pit was on the south side of the churchyard, and, it was rumoured, a certain Bishop of Carlisle had a cock pit in the garden of Rose Castle. However, in 1909 this was claimed to be nothing more sinister than a sunken garden. Perhaps, perhaps...

cock spurs were usually steel, though occasionally silver, spikes mounted on leather gauntlets which fitted over the natural spurs

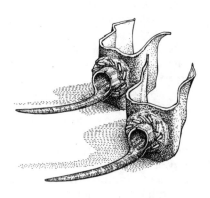

A pair of cock spurs.

of a fighting cock. With these, the bird could inflict vicious wounds on its opponent. (see **cockfighting**)

cock walk part of the farmyard where cocks were kept and prepared for fighting. *Cock o' the walk* referred to someone in in a prominent and influential position: *'Aye, he's dressed up like cock o' t' walk'*.

cocks and hens sycamore blossom

cofe calf. In the 1840s, when the Ordnance Survey cartographers were drafting their maps of Furness and Cartmel, they asked local people the names of certain features. Not being able to understand the dialect, this resulted in an area of Walney Island being labelled 'Cove o' Kend'; in fact the correct name was 'Cofe Hook End'! How many more of our placenames have been irrevocably altered in this way?

cofe lick tuft of hair on the forehead that will not part or lie flat. The hair of a calf (*cofe*) or cow remains for some time in the direction of the last licking by the animal's tongue.

colliers charcoal burners

collops slices of dried or smoked meat

Collop Monday the Monday before Lent when *collops* (qv) were eaten before the beginning of the Lenten fast. William Fleming, the Furness diarist, recorded on the 10th February 1812:

It is customary in this corner of England on this day for most families to dine on dried meat cut into thin slices and fried with eggs, from which custom it is vulgarly called Collop Monday

come *It will be ten years come August* means it will be ten years when August has arrived

coming round the act of recovery from an illness *Ah's bin badly but ah'm coming round now*

con squirrel. The place-name Ickenthwaite is derived from this word, and means 'the clearing where squirrels are found' (ON *ik-orni*, squirrel)

The con.

conny (Furness), **canny**[1] term of praise meaning nice, attractive, pleasant. The same word is in common use in the north-east of England.

conny, canny[2] cautious *Go canny wi' cream!*

coo-as term used in West Cumbria for the building in which cows are kept. In central and north Cumbria the word used is *byre*; while *shippon* is more common in the south of the county. (see also *dobby stones*, *fodder-gang*, *rud stake*)

Cookson, Isaac from Gillhead, Bampton, was a well-known shepherd in the eastern Lakeland fells.

Isaac Cookson and a Herdwick 'yowe'.

He is known to have attended the *Mardale Shepherds' Meet* (qv) on sixty-four occasions. In the late twentieth century he has become something of a romantic cult figure, and his genial image appears on postcards, tea-towels and in motorway service stations.

cop to catch *Tha'll cop it when yer fadder gets home!* ie retribution will follow

coppy steàl low wooden stool (N *kubbe stol*, a small stool made from a log)

corkers (see *caulkers*)

corkin' a very severe beating *he got a reet corkin'!*

Corp Co op (see *divi day*)

corpse roads In remote Cumbrian dales, chapels often did not have the right to bury members of the local community, and bodies had to be transported on crude sleds or on the backs of packhorses to distant churches along *corpse roads*. One of the best known of these runs over Burnmoor from Wasdale Head to Boot in the neighbouring valley of Eskdale, and visitors to St Catherine's Church will find a number of gravestones commemorating people who died at Wasdale Head. (see also *corpse ways*)

corpse ways jealously-guarded routes from farms to the church along which corpses were carried for burial, any deviation being regarded as an ill-omen. In Troutbeck (Westmorland) there are records of fences being removed to allow a funeral procession to pass along a traditional route.

corve circular or oval basket, made of hazel rods, which was used to carry coal in Cumbrian mines

costrel small cask or barrel, Often used at *clippin' time* (qv) to hold *ruddle* (qv) (see *tar costrel*)

coul dragging up cockles from the sand using a rake (Cartmel peninsula) (see also *cramb, hardbacks, jumbo, skeear, teanal, wheaat*)

country dances Cumbrian dances included the *Cumberland Square Eight*, the *Long Eight, Ninepins Reel*, the *Circassian Circle* and the *Cushion Dance* (qv) — similar in many respects to Scottish country dancing, a point which did not escape John Keats when he visited Ireby in 1818:

> ... *the difference between our country dances and these Scotch figures is about the same as leisurely stirring a cup o' Tea and beating up a batter pudding*

coup muck cart

court cupboards (see *bread cupboards*)

'cow and worm' kettle and coil condenser used in the distilling of illicit whisky. The term for such nefarious activity was *milkin' coos in t' haystacks*. (see Slee, Lanty)

cow clog large piece of wood to hang around the neck of a cow to prevent it *loupin'* (qv) *t' dyke* (cf *sheep sime*)

cowm, coom, comb dust and debris of peat

cowp to exchange, to trade, to barter. Copeland, a division of West Cumbria, is believed to be 'bought land'.

cowp't ower collapsed, fainted, fallen over

coze house house in which a corpse has been laid out prior to burial (see *laying out*, *streek*)

crab wild apple (see *Egremont Crab Fair*)

crack[1] chat, conversation *Ah wer just hevvin' a lile crack wi' me marrer* (qv)

crack[2] to boast, to brag, to praise *it's not all it's cracked up to be*

crag-fast stranded on a ledge or *bink* (qv) of rock from which it is impossible to ascend or descend

cramb hooked fork used in cockling (see also *coul*, *hardbacks*, *jumbo*, *skeear*, *teanal*, *wheaat*)

cramp bone patella bone of a sheep or a lamb worn as a charm against cramp (cf *lucky bone*)

cranch to crush or grind with the teeth

cravick't stiff in the joints and muscles *Ah'm fair cravick't*

cree to crush or break into fragments, to soak oatmeal etc

creean moaning noise made by animals (Scottish *croon*, a long moan)

criam small metal staple used to mend a crack in a wooden bowl or dish

Crier of Claife This spine-chilling legend concerns a ghostly and misguided delinquent who, especially on dark nights, unexpectedly hailed the Windermere ferryman from the Westmorland shore. On one occasion, the ferryman who answered the summons returned with an empty boat, horror-stricken and dumb, in which state he died a few days later. Present-day ferry passengers on the *Mallard* need have no fear, for the story goes on to relate how monks from Furness Abbey exorcised this troublesome individual and he is supposed to be buried on Claife Heights.

cringle curved; Crinkle Crags are the fells which circle the head of Great Langdale (I *kringla*, a circle)

crones, creanns cranberries (cf *mossberries*)

crooks Next to his dog, the shepherd's best friend is his stick or crook. They are usually made of hazel gathered at the **back end**

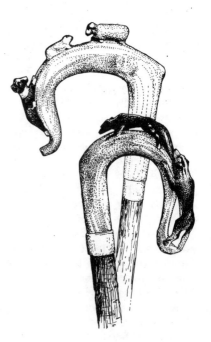

The carving of crooks or sticks is a Cumbrian art-form.

(qv) and allowed to season for a year or so. The crook handle is made from ram's horn shaped by boiling it until it becomes pliable, and then carved into a variety of shapes such as hounds, foxes, rabbits, thistles etc. Finally it is browned over with a hot iron and polished.

*Whee-ivva thoo is, owdther
   thin er else fat —*
*Thoo maut gang awae till
   thoos shutten this yat!*
or — if unfamiliar with the vernacular:
   Kindly close the gate
cross buttock   move in Cumberland and Westmorland **wrestling**

A guide stone in Cartmel marks the Cross Sands route over Morecambe Bay.

cropper   nasty fall *Ah came a reet cropper on a slape* (qv) *stane*
Crosby Ravensworth Fell   The gate leading onto the fell has this dialect inscription:
   *Gederen thi yows up, or laiten
      t' beeas in,*
   *Whaerivva thoo's gaan,
      whaerivva thoos bin,*

(qv), meaning to get an opponent into such a position as to be able to throw him over the hip by using the buttock as a fulcrum
Crossthat   Crosthwaite
Cross Sands route   An ancient routeway across the sands of Morecambe Bay at low water. Probably used back in the Bronze Age, in

medieval times it was one of the most important routes into Cumbria from the south, and Robert Bruce used it in 1322 to make a surprise attack on Lancaster. It failed to impress John Wesley on his missionary trips to West Cumberland, but Wordsworth used it frequently — indeed he heard the news of the death of Robespierre from fellow travellers in the middle of the bay. Because of the shortness of the distance between Ulverston and Lancaster — a mere 22 miles (35km) as opposed to 34 miles (54km) around the estuaries of the Kent and Leven — and despite the dangerous quicksands, the route remained in regular use until 1857, when the Ulverston to Carnforth railway line was opened. (see *brobbs*)

Crosthwaite, Peter Describing himself as 'Admiral of the Keswick Regatta, Keeper of the Museum at Keswick, Guide, Pilot, Geographer and Hydrographer to the Nobility and Gentry', Peter Crosthwaite (1735–1808) was one of those larger-than-life eighteenth century eccentrics on a par with **Joseph Pocklington** (qv). As a former captain of an East India Company vessel, he knew the art of marine surveying, and his maps of the main lakes were the most accurate of their time and eagerly bought by the early tourists. His museum in Keswick Market place was highly regarded — but not by all. One Cambridge undergraduate, William Gell, recorded with commendable candour in 1797 :

His collection chiefly consists of mineral productions and those indian bows, caps and ornaments which are to be found in every museum ... His daughter is an elegant woman and more worth seeing than anything else in his house ...

crowdy form of soup in which the stock from boiling meat was poured over oatmeal (see *hasty pudding*, *poddish*)

crucks (see *siles*)

crud curd

cruddy, crudger small clay marble (see *taws[1]*)

cruel extreme, excessive *a cruel lang time*

crum horn't horns turned towards the eyes

cubble For fishing purposes, Windermere was divided into three sections known the *High*, *Middle* and *Low cubble*. The origin of the word is obscure.

cuckoo bread and cheese leaves and flowers of the wood sorrel

cuddy donkey or ass *'Hes ta ivver seen a cuddy loup* (qv) *a five barr'd yat* (qv)?' *'Aye, it mun* (qv) *hae been a gay* (qv) *lish* (qv) *cuddy else a varra laal yat!'*

cult objects Certain trees were thought to posses mystical powers — eg the **rowan** (qv), but, in some areas, oak trees near to wells or springs were decorated with broken crockery or coloured rags on Maundy Thursday. Stones, too, could be powerful charms (see *dobby stones*), and at **Urswick** (qv) a large limestone boulder, the Priapus Stone, was decorated with sheep *salve*, coloured rags and flowers on Midsummer Day, presumably as a votive offering in anticipation of a good harvest. The stone still exists — though its powers of fecundity are apparently no longer required ...

Cumberland and Westmorland Antiquarian and Archaeological Society Founded in 1866, the CWAAS is one of the most respected antiquarian and archaeological societies in the country. As well as covering the two counties named, it also embraces Furness and Cartmel which, until 1974, were part of Lancashire. The *Old Series* of annual transactions ran from 1866 to 1900; the *New Series* from 1901 to the present.

Cumberland and Westmorland wrestling (see **wrestling**)

Cumberland sausage (see *Waberthwaite Cumberland sausage*)

Cumbrian sickle usually about 2 feet 6 inches (75cm) long, it had saw teeth, fifteen every inch, rather than a sharp, smooth blade

cumd'y-gard'y come day, go day, easy-going

cush, cush call to cows for milking

cushat wood pigeon

cushion dance form of ring dance in which a young man lays

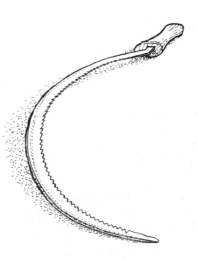

A Cumbrian sickle.

a cushion at the feet of a girl; both then kneel on the cushion and kiss, accompanied by a squealing fiddle. The girl takes the cushion to another partner who also kisses her and later leaves her free to link with the first partner. The process is continued until the whole group is involved and they all form a circle. Beats disco dancing ... (see *country dances*)

cut bearing, demeanour; *the cut of his jib* refers to the face or appearance of a person

D

daad slight covering of snow *a laal* (qv) *daad o' snow on t' fell'* (cf *greymin*)

Dacre bears four mysterious stones in St Andrew's churchyard. The legend relates that, anticlockwise from the north-west, the first is asleep with its head on a pillar, the second is attacked by a cat, the third bear tries to shake off its adversary, while the fourth bear solves the problem by eating the cat! It seems possible that the bears were once part of the battlements of the nearby Dacre Castle.

daft ha'p'orth (ie halfpenny worth) said, without malice, to a foolish child or person (possibly from OE *gedaefte*, meek, mild)

daggy wet and misty weather

dales larnin' Education has long been prized in Cumbria. As well as ancient grammar schools at Penrith, Ulverston, St Bees, Bampton, Hawkshead and elsewhere, certain enlightened gentlemen and farmers passed on their knowledge of mathematics and languages to keen pupils. The blind philosopher, mathematician and botanist **John Gough** (qv) tutored the young **John Dalton** (qv), while **John Barrow** (qv) was taught mathematics and astronomy by William Gibson, a Cartmel 'wise man', and **'Wonderful' Walker** (qv) was taught Latin by a gentleman living in Dunnerdale. Even in remote areas, a classical education was not uncommon. The story is told of a group of nineteenth century undergraduates staying at an inn in the Whicham Valley (though another version sets it in Eskdale) who loudly called for their bill to be made up in Latin; within minutes the bill appeared — in Latin, in Greek and in Hebrew! (see **Fallows, Fearon, Otley, Jonathan,** *Willy o' th' Hollins*)

dalt, dote stone wall or fence made and repaired by various parties with common rights (see **drystone walls, wall head**)

Dalton, John (1766–1844) Less than eighteen miles (29km) from the towers of Sellafield lies the West Cumbrian village of Eaglesfield where John Dalton, the originator of the atomic theory, was born. Although he left school at the age of ten, he became skilled in mathematics and languages (see *dales larnin'*). His passion for meteorology took him to the summit of Helvellyn on forty occasions in order to measure the dew point. He was appointed to the Chair of Mathematics and Philosophy at New College, Manchester where, at the age of thirty-eight, he astonished the scientific world with his theory of atomic weights. In addition he investigated the phenomenon known as colour blindness, a condition with which he was afflicted.

Dalton, Millican (see **hermits**)

dander temper *Aye, he's got 'is dander up*

darrak, dargue a day's work; a *darrak o' peat* was the amount of fuel a man could cut from a *peat pot* (qv) in one day (ON *dagverk*, a day's work)

daub to plaster with mortar or mud (see *clay daubin*)

daup, dawp carrion crow

daubment any kind of ointment or oil applied to the skin to assist healing; also used disparagingly as a term for women's make-up

Davie, William Richardson born in Egremont on the 22nd June 1756. With his parents, Archibald and Mary, he emigrated to the American colonies. He ultimately became a lawyer, and in this capacity he was at the Congress in 1787 which drew up the Constitution of the fledgling United States.

dead tongue water hemlock (Furness area)

deaf nuts nuts without kernels or with unsound kernels in the shells (cf *St John's nut*, *St Mary's nut*); *he cracks no deaf nuts* was said of well-fed persons or animals

deal a large amount *he left a deal o' debt*

Deans, Mrs Charlotte Born in Wigton, Charlotte Deans *née* Lowe (1768-1859) became a 'barnstormer' or itinerant actress in her twenties. Although her name does not appear on any known playbills and she never became famous outside Cumbria and southern Scotland, this flamboyant character wrote her autobiography which chronicles the almost Dickensian trials and vicissitudes of a life spent 'on the boards'. Apart from producing seventeen children for her two husbands, William Johnston and Thomas

A daup.

The Devil's Bridge at Kirkby Lonsdale is supposed to have been built by 'auld Nick' himself.

Deans, she performed in barns, stables and makeshift 'theatres' throughout the length and breadth of Cumbria — a remarkable lady and one of life's great survivors. (see **theatres**)

deck   to dress in a precise way *all decked out in his Sunday best*

deef   deaf

deet   to separate grain from the chaff (see *flail, weyt*)

deg   to dampen, to sprinkle water on anything (I *döggva*, ON *doegva*, to moisten, to sprinkle)

delve   (see *grave*)

dench   squeamish, delicate

despart   painful

Devil's Bridge   The bridge at Kirkby Lonsdale is traditionally said to have been built by none other than **auld Nick** himself. The legend says that an old woman's cow strayed across the River Lune and was stranded on the far bank. The Devil appeared and charmingly agreed to build a bridge so that the old lady could cross and regain her cow. The price — naturally — was the soul of the first living thing to cross the bridge. The following morning the old woman returned to inspect the bridge, now complete, and setting down a small dog, threw across the bridge a titbit, which the animal duly followed, whereupon the Devil disappeared with a howl of rage. The marks of his fingers may still be seen on one of the coping stones. In fact the bridge was probably built in the late fifteenth century by monks of St Mary's Abbey, York. (see also **Simon's Nick**)

Devil's snuff box   common puffball fungus (cf *fuz ball*)

deyke   (see *dyke*)

dez'd   cold and stiff

dibbler   pewter plate

dickey   hedge sparrow

Dick's hat band   (see *queer as Dick's hat band*)

diddle   to deceive   *Ah were fair diddled*

dike   (see *dyke*)

dinge   to dent   *tha's dinged t' bucket*

dip   hot bacon fat

dip cakes   fried bread

dish   cup   *sit thee doon and hev a dish o' tea*. Possibly derived from the habit — not yet extinct — of drinking tea from a saucer to cool it.

dista?   see *dusta?*

divi day   day on which a dividend on purchases could be claimed from the Co-operative Wholesale Society. A society membership number had to be quoted on each visit to the *Corp*, and the mantra 'sixteen-four-twelve' is a lasting part of the the author's childhood. *He's so lucky that if he fell off t' Co-op he'd land in t' divi!*

do   feast, celebration, *merry neet* (qv)   *it were a grand do tudder neet*

doake   mark made by a *fluke* (qv) where it has lain on the sand (Cartmel)

dobbers   (see *bobbers*)

dobby   ghost, apparition (see *dobby stones*)

dobby stones   naturally-holed stones strung on a string which were hung over the heads of cattle in a *byre* to prevent the bewitching of the animals by the *evil eye* (qv) (cf *holy-stones*) (see **witchcraft**)

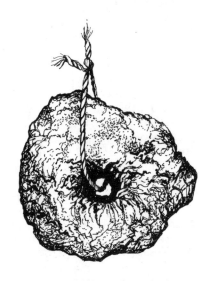

A dobby stone was a powerful charm against witchcraft.

dockin   common dock. Traditionally used as a cure for nettle stings when rubbed over the affected part with the words *dockin in, nettle out* repeated three times.

doctor   to mend or patch   *T' poke's* (qv) *brossen* (qv) *but ah doctored it wi' string*

Doctor's Bridge   This bridge in Eskdale began as a **packhorse bridge** (qv) and the evidence may be see underneath the structure. It appears that in 1734 the resident doctor, Dr Edward Tyson, acquired a horse and trap which could not negotiate the narrow packhorse bridge, and consequently he had it widened — hence the name.

Dodd Man George Smith, the Skiddaw Hermit (qv) (see **hermits**)

dodder, dadder to shake, to quiver *me legs is reet doddery*

dog part of a rainbow (Furness)

A rainbow in the morning
Is the shepherd's warning;
A dog in the night
Is the sailor's delight

meaning that part of a rainbow seen before sunset is the precursor of fine weather

dog fall term used in Cumberland and Westmorland **wrestling** (qv) when both contestants fall and neither can be declared the victor

dogstinks dandelion (cf *pissibed*)

dog-whippers men appointed by a parish to clear dogs from churches during the service. At Waberthwaite in 1605 four 'sydmen' (sidesmen) were appointed 'to keep dogges out of the chirche', and parishes as diverse as Crosby Ravensworth, Dalston, Penrith, Ulverston, Torpenhow and Hawkshead all had their *dog-whippers*. In Wordsworth's time, the grammar school lads used to amuse themselves by smuggling dogs into Hawkshead Church, an act which did not endear them to John 'Pharaoh' Pepper, the local *dog-whipper*. After he reported the matter to the schoolmaster, the boys were obliged to make amends by leaving the price of a quart of ale for him at the local hostelry.

dolly blue or ultramarine was made in a former cotton mill at Backbarrow on the River Leven from the 1890s to 1981. The process involved the heating of sulphur, pitch, china clay and soda ash in large kilns, and the

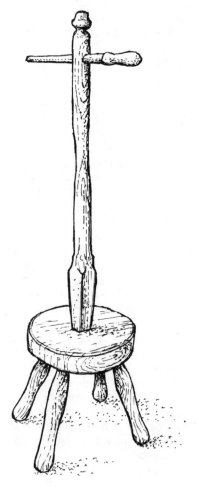

Dolly legs.

EVERY HOUSEWIFE SHOULD USE

Donkey Stone takes its name from the brand.

resulting blue powder was used in a variety of industrial processes, as well as being packaged in small sachets which were dipped in the rinsing water in order to whiten cotton clothes. The building is now the fashionable Whitewater Hotel, but some of the outbuildings nearby still have traces of ultramarine in their walls, indicating their former use.

dolly legs, dolly wooden implement resembling a four-legged stool on a long wooden handle. Used for agitating clothes when washing in a *dolly tub*. (see *posser*)

don a marble (see *taws¹*)

donk moist, damp, dank; a *donky day* means a wet day (D *dönke*, to moisten)

donkey rake (see *nag rake*)

Donkey stone white or yellow stone used for colouring door steps and the area immediately in front of the step. The name is derived from the trade name Read's Donkey Brand. These stones were usually given away by the *rag-and-bone man* (qv) in exchange for old clothes.

donnat, donnet Devil (cf *auld Nick*); unruly person or animal

47

donnocks marbles knocked out of the circle by an opponent (see *taws[1]*)

dookers bathing suit, swimwear (W Cumbria)

douker diving duck

dowly melancholy, dismal, lonely (I *dauflegur*, lonely, sad)

down house service area of a farmhouse, usually approached down a few steps. Here the washing and brewing would be undertaken and here, too, the *elding* (qv) would be stored. (see *fire house*)

downbanks descending, downhill (as opposed to **upbanks**, ascending, uphill)

draff malt grains after brewing

dree slow, tedious, dreary *Ah got it done at last but it were a varra dree job* (D *droi*, tedious)

drenching horn usually a large cow horn in which potions were mixed and poured into an animal's throat. In Great Langdale in the 1920s, pigs were **drenched** with an old boot with the toe removed!

dress to prepare; to put in order; to winnow grain. A *clock dresser* was a clock mender.

dressing brake iron bar on which the *river* (qv) placed slate[1] (qv) and shaped it with a *whittle* (qv) (see also *plug-and-feather*)

drinkin' mid-morning refreshment

drubbin' a thrashing *Ah'll gi' thee a good drubbin'!*

Drunken Duck Inn originally called the Barngates Inn, Hawkshead, the pub is said to have acquired its name from a duck which passed out after imbibing too freely from a barrel of ale which had burst in the inn yard. The thrifty landlady, assuming the bird to be a deceased duck, plucked it for the pot, but fortunately it revived and waddled out into the yard uttering intoxicated quacking noises. In a fit of remorse the landlady knitted a woolly vest for the bird.

The drunken duck which gave its name to the inn at Hawkshead.

dry thirsty *Ah'm reet dry*

dry dyke (see *whick dyke*)

dryope quivering of distant sand in the heat of a summer's day (Cartmel)

drystone walls Most of Lakeland's **drystone walls** are, in fact, double walls tied together 'like Cumberland and Westmorland champion wrestlers' (Norman Nicholson) with *through stones* (qv). Built on *footings* (qv), the gap in the middle is filled with *hearting stones* (qv) and the wall is finished off with a line of *cam stones* (qv). The majority of **drystone walls** which snake and flow over the highest Cumbrian fells were built between 1750 and 1850. There are, of course, exceptions, such as the thirteenth century turf and stone wall in upper Eskdale which was built by the monks of Furness Abbey to enclose their sheep pasture, or the boundary

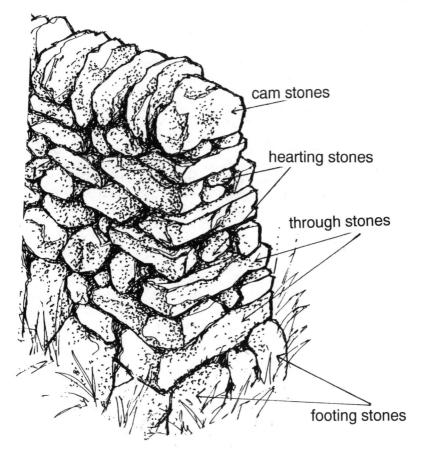

cam stones

hearting stones

through stones

footing stones

A characteristic Lakeland drystone wall. 'Yan on twa an twa on yan' was one of the secrets of a good wall.

wall of 1551 between the townships of Ambleside and Troutbeck which runs along the side of Red Screes, but the rule of thumb holds good. At the end of the eighteenth century, a rood of seven and a half yards (7m) of **drystone wall** some five and a half feet (1.5m) high could be built for between one shilling and six pence and one shilling and eight pence. The builders were often illiterate and could sign their wage receipts only wth a cross — but they have left their signature all over the fells for us to see and admire to this day. (see also *batter*, *bearded wall*, *bee boles*, *bellying*, *hogg-holes*, *rabbit smoot*, *rush*, *wall head*)

dub pool or deep water in a beck. Sheepfolds are often found near to *dubs*, reflecting the fact that sheep were often washed before they were *clipped* (qv) (cf *lum*) (I *djúpur*, deep)

Duck Apple Night Hallowe'en, when apples were floated in a large bowl of water and children attempted to sieze them with their teeth. Alternatively, the apples would be dangled from strings. (see *bobbing the apple*, *Hanshin' Neet*)

duck wine water

ducks wi' veils on (see *savery ducks*)

ducksten game played with round stones (*ducks*). One stone is placed on a large flat stone (*ducksten*), the aim being to knock it off by pitching the other stones. In Wigton the game was known as *ducky*.

dummack rounded heap or hummock; heaps of manure in fields ready for spreading

Dunmail said to be the last Celtic king of Cumbria. When Edmund, king of the Anglians, invaded the area in AD 945, Dunmail was defeated at a great battle on the raise or pass which bears his name. The legend claims that he is buried under the great cairn on the summit of the pass, and that his followers threw his crown into Grisedale Tarn to prevent it falling into the hands of his enemy. Sadly, this story from the 'Celtic twilight' does not withstand scutiny; Dunmail died in Rome on a pilgrimage thirty years or so after his defeat, and the great cairn is probably no more than a boundary marker.

dunsh to bump into something; a butt delivered by a sheep or a cow

dust to physically chastise, used figuratively as in **Ah'll dust thi jacket!**; also an uproar, a scandal *he kicked up a reet old dust*

dusta?, dista? do you? *Dusta kna t' road to Kezzick?*

D'ye ken John Peel? sung wherever the English language is spoken. The words are by John Woodcock Graves of Wigton, who is reported to have told Peel '... you'll be sung when we're both run to earth' — and such was the case. The original dialect version of the first stanza ran:

Did ye ken John Peel wid his cwote sae grey?
did ye ken John Peel at the breck o' day?
did ye ken John Peel gayin' far, far away—

*Wie his hoons and his horn in
   a mwornin'?*

Chorus:

*For the sound o' the horn
   caw'd me fra my bed
As the cry o' the hoons me
   often has led,
For Peel's view holla wad
   waken the dead,
Or a fox frae his lair in a
   mwornin'*

The present music, based on an
old air, was written by William
Metcalfe in 1868. (see **hodden
grey**, Peel, John, *Tally Ho! Tally
Ho! Follow the Hounds*)

Dyer, Jimmy (1841-1903) was
well-known in the Carlisle area as
an itinerant fiddler and ballad
singer. His statue stands in the
Lanes shopping development,
Carlisle. (see **fiddlers, Wells, Benjamin, Stagg, John**)

dyke, deyke, dike a hedge or
wall. *'A double-rank stone dyke'*
(Norman Nicholson) (see **drystone
walls**, *liggers*, *whick dyke*)

E

eaa the channel of a stream on the foreshore at low water; a river, hence the River Eea in Cartmel (I á, as in *Hvitá*, the White River)

eagle rope In the eighteenth century, eagles were feared predators of lambs and therefore they were destroyed as vermin. A long rope, kept in Borrowdale but also used by the inhabitants of Buttermere, Ennerdale, Langdale and Eskdale, allowed men to be lowered down to an eyrie to destroy the eggs.

eaned, heant possessing a strong taste, like meat going bad

earles (see *arles*)

earnest money (see *arles*)

Easterledge pudding Made and eaten in spring, *Easterledge* or *herb pudding* consisted of the leaves of bistort, called *Easterledges* in Cumbria, young nettles, one or two blackcurrant leaves, a few blades of chives and a handful of groats or barley, all boiled in a *puddin' poke* or linen bag. Before serving it was customary to add a little butter and a beaten egg. It is still eaten today and is regarded as *good fer thi blood*.

Easterma giants Easterledges or bistort (see *Easterledge pudding*)

Eat up — yer at yer aunty's urban expression — mainly Barrow — possibly imported from

Easterma giants.

Lancashire. It is simply an encouragement to eat heartily and without restraint.

ebben (often pron *ebm*) even, equal to, in line with

ebben-up-an-doon straight, honest fellow, one who can be trusted

eck (see *end board*)

edderful angry, revengeful

eddle to earn (cf *addle*, *yaddle*)

edge appetite *Nay, ah've nobbut* (qv) *a poor edge on fer mi dinner*

edgrow, eddish aftermath; second crop of grass after mowing. Often spelled 'eatgrowe' in seventeenth century court rolls. (cf *efter-crop*)

Edmondson, Thomas After the failure of his cabinet-making business in Carlisle, Thomas Edmondson (1792- 1851) joined the Newcastle and Carlisle Railway Company and became station master at Brampton, where he invented the first mechanised printed rail ticket system, which was still in use until comparatively recently.

een eyes *Een as black as sloes* (OE *eagan*, eyes)

efter-crop second crop, grown after the first one has been harvested (cf *edgrow*)

efter-temsings coarse flour after sifting

egg (see *pace eggs*)

egg, egg on to invite, to urge on; *egg-battle* is one who urges others to quarrel and fight (ON *eggja*, to stimulate)

Egremont Crab Fair Apart from the two World Wars, the fair has been held since 1267 when Thomas de Multon, Lord of Egremont,

granted a charter to hold a fair on the nearest Saturday to the 19th September. Apples — originally crab-apples — are distributed to spectators, hence the name, and the World *gurning* (qv) championships are held.

Egremont, The Horn of The legend relates that two Lucy brothers, Eustace and Hubert, joined a crusade. On leaving Egremont Castle, Eustace, as the rightful heir, blew the horn hanging in the gateway but instructed his brother that if he fell in battle, Hubert was to return, blow the horn, and claim the estate. One version of the story says that Eustace was taken prisoner by the Saracens, and Hubert returned to Egremont and claimed the estate — but was unable to blow the horn. One day the castle rang to the sound of the horn — Eustace had returned to claim his birthright, and Hubert fled in disgrace. Inevitably, Wordsworth wrote a poem about this brotherly treachery, *The Horn of Egremont Castle*, and today the name of a pub — the Horn — commemorates the story.

eish, esh ash trees; *eish-chats* are the seeds of the ash tree

If t' esh tree buds afoor
t' yak (qv),
T' following summer will be
black,
But if t' yak buds titter (qv)
cummer
'Tis sewer to be a drufty [fine]
summer (ancient rhyme)

Before the Agricultural Revolution, ash leaves were carefully harvested and used as winter food for the few sheep kept through the winter. In the seventeenth century the court baron of the Manor of Windermere made it an offence to 'cutt down or breake any other Men's Ash leaves', a clear indication of their value. (OE *aesce*, ash)

Eish or esh.

elding fuel (I, ON *eldur*, fire)

elf shot Even as late as the eighteenth century, it was believed that both humans and animals could be shot and killed by elves using tiny flint arrowheads. The belief probably originated in Scandinavia and it is mentioned in the *Bandamanna Saga*. A cure was possible if the victim was touched with another elf arrow or given water in which such an arrow had been washed. Clearly, such arrows were highly prized, and this possibly accounts for the entry in Bishop Nicolson's diary for the 27th June 1712, in which he claims to have visited the Bowness-on-Solway area and seen 'several Elf Arrows too pretious [sic] ... to be parted with'.

ellers alder trees (I *elri*, OE *eldra*, alder trees)

elliker (see *alegar*)

end board removable board at the rear of a farm cart (qv) (cf *heck¹*, *skut¹*)

end nor side Cumbrian version of 'head nor tail' *He cud nowther mek end nor side on't*

enoo enough *there's enoo on* (qv) *us*

erchin (see *urchin*)

Eshd'l Eskdale

esslins salmon fry before they go to sea

ether common snake or adder (cf *hag worm*) (north-east Cumbria)

etwixt between *it's my dike etwixt girt stane an' yak*

everly constantly

evil eye much feared, even as late as the seventeenth and eighteenth centuries. Horseshoes or two crossed straws were often fixed to the *threshwood* (qv) of farmhouses to prevent the malignant influence, and *dobby stones* (qv) were hung in *byres* to prevent the cattle being bewitched. (see **witchcraft**)

ex, ax to ask

exings the banns of marriage

ey up! look out! watch out!

F

fadder father

faddy fussy, particular *he's faddy about his food*

fail to decline in health *she's failing fast*

fair completely, absolutely *Ah fair dreaded visitin' t' dentist*

fair do's to share equally among a group

fain pleased, glad *Ah's fain to see thee agin* (I *feginn*, pleased, glad)

fairin' present from the fair

fallal gaudy items of clothing, finery, trumpery

T' lasses irn't hoaf sa smart
For o' the'r fallal hats an' veils

Ben Wells, poem by A C Gibson

Fallows, Fearon Born in the house next to that in which William Wordsworth was born eighteen years before, Fearon Fallows (1788–1831) was the son of a weaver, a trade he entered until aged nineteen or twenty, when he became a schoolteacher at Plumbland. His ability in mathematics and algebra in particular earned him a place at St John's College, Cambridge, and later a lectureship in mathematics at Corpus Christi College. In 1821 Fallows sailed for the Cape of Good Hope, where he established the observatory there and made a significant contribution to astronomy. One nineteenth century writer said of him: 'As a mathematician and general scholar, Fallows was the greatest man Cockermouth has produced. His knowledge of algebra approached the marvellous'. (see *dales larnin'*)

famish famous *he's a famish russler* (qv)

fan-teckled, farmatickled freckled

farlies, farleys strange, wondrous sights

farm carts By the late eighteenth century, light wooden farm carts had replaced the heavy, cumbersome carts with *clog wheels* (qv). These new vehicles had two dished spoked wheels and could be drawn by a single horse, and the capacity could be increased by the use of *overings* (qv). (see also *end board*)

fash trouble, bother, worry *Don't fash thissen* (qv) (Romany word)

Fasnas Eve, Fassen's Even, Fasten Eve Fastings Eve, ie Shrove Tuesday

The Fatal Nuptual poem, most probably written by Richard

A Cumbrian farm cart.

Braithwaite of Burneside Hall, which chronicles the disaster which took place on the 19th October 1635 when the Windermere ferryboat sank. On board were 48 or 49 wedding guests and eight horses returning from a celebration at Hawkshead, but there is no evidence that the bride and groom were on board. All the victims were buried at St Martin's Church, Bowness.

fat's in t' fire, the mischief or trouble has commenced

favour resembles, has the appearance of *he favours his fadder* (qv)

feast er famine either a surfeit or a paucity of something

feckless incompetent, feeble, useless

fell mountain or high hill
London for riches, Preston for pride
Kendal for poverty on the fell-side
                   local rhyme
(I, N, S *fjell*, mountain)

fellanders eighteenth century expression for those who live within the fells

fell-faa, fell-fo fieldfare

fellies, felloes curved segments making up the circumference of a wooden wheel (see *naff*)

fell in wi' met by chance *Ah fell in wi' me marra* (qv) *fra Workiton* (qv)

fell running relatively new sport in which the competitor pits himself against the clock. It calls for a degree of stamina, courage and confidence which very few outdoor activities demand. (see **Naylor, Joss**)

fellon-wood bitter-sweet

fend to provide, to earn a living *he can fend fer hissel* (qv) *now*

ferry, firry used by children to select the first turn in any game (see also *bags*, *laggy*)

festing penny money given to a servant on hiring to bind the agreement. Possibly from fastening money. (cf *arles*, *earles*, *earnest money*, *yarles*)

fettle to fit, to put in order, to make ready, to set right; *in fine fettle* means in good order or condition. (I *fella* [pron *fettla*], to put in order)

few an unspecified quantity *a girt few*, *a laal few*

fiddlers Most dales could boast at least one **fiddler** to provide music for *merry neets* (qv). Hugh Walpole's description in *Rogue Herries* of 'old Johnny Shoestring

Fiddlers usually provided music for 'merry neets', but also led bridal couples to church.

in bright blue breeches with silver buckles to his shoes, perched on a high stool fiddling for his life' is not far off the mark. In addition, fiddlers often played ahead of the happy couple as they walked to the church for their wedding, a custom which still prevails in parts of Norway to this day. (see **Wells, Benjamin, Stagg, John, Dyer, Jimmy**)

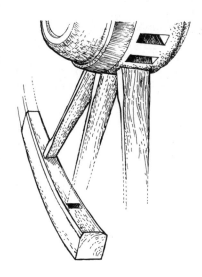

Ash fellies were the curved segments making up the rim of a cart wheel; the naff or hub was usually elm, and the spokes were oak.

fidge   to be restless, a restless person

Fiend's Fell   traditional name for Cross Fell, the highest point in the Pennines

fig sue, fig sewe   figs stewed with ale and seasoned with sugar and spices. William Fleming, the Furness yeoman farmer, declared in 1810:

'... it has been an immemorial custom in this corner of England, on Good Friday, to eat a kind of porridge, called here fig sewe, made of figs cut in quarters, with wheaten bread cut into small square pieces and boiled in ale or beer seasoned with sugar or treacle and nutmeg'

Filly Fair   At Arlecdon in West Cumbria, Palm Sunday was once regarded as a day for sport and recreation; it was known as Filly Fair but the origin of the term is unknown

findy   plump, weighty, solid, firm, of substance

A cold May and windy
Makes a fat barn and findy
     Westmorland weather rhyme

Finsthwaite 'Princess'   A simple marble cross, erected in 1913 in the churchyard at Finsthwaite near the southern end of Windermere, marks the grave of Clementina Johannes Sobieski Douglas of Waterside, buried here on the 16th May 1771. A former vicar, Canon C G Townley, and others were convinced that she was the illegitimate daughter of Prince Charles Edward Stuart, the Young Pretender, and Clementina Walkinshaw. Prince Charles's mother was Princess Maria Clementina, granddaughter of King John Sobiesky of Poland. Moreover, in 1760 Miss Walkinshaw, in a letter to the Old Pretender's secretary writes: '... before 1745 I lived in London [and] was between then and 1747 undone ...', which Canon Townley took to mean the birth of an illegitimate child. Was this daughter brought up in this remote corner of Cumbria in order to conceal her true identity? Was she of Royal blood? The mystery remains.

fire crane   a pivoted device mounted at one side of the fire, from which **rattencrooks** (qv) were suspended

fire cults   (see hearth cults)

fire house   main living accommodation in a farm. Often simply called the 'house', this room contained the main fire.

fire window   small window designed to allow light to fall directly on the hearth. Many *fire windows* were blocked up to avoid paying the window tax, since they were usually the smallest windows in the house.

firry   (see *ferry*)

fish stones   large flat stones in the market place, on which fish was exposed for sale. There are good examples in Cartmel and Broughton.

fisslen about   dashing about *t' moose was fisslen aboot t' bedroom* (cf *pintallin'*)

flaach, flaitch   one who induces by flattery; one who cajoles; to induce by flattery, to wheedle, to

coax (OE *fleech*, to beseech)
flae   to frighten (cf *flairt*)
flail   simple threshing implement. A *swingle* (qv) of holly wood was attached to a long ash-pole by means of an eel-skin thong. *Flailing* was usually done by two men who maintained a steady rhythm as the *swingle* threshed the grain, separating the grain from the husks. (see also *berrier*, *deet*)

Flailing grain.

flags   thin slabs of stone or **slate**[1] (qv) used as paving stones. The geological term **Brathay Flags** describes a specific type of slate. Flag Street in Hawkshead is so named because a small *syke* (qv) was covered with *flags*.

flairt, flaet   frightened, alarmed (cf *flae*)
flay-crow, flay-scarl   scarecrow

A flay-crow or flay-scarl.

flaysome   hideous or frightful *What's ta mekkin' that flaysome din fer?*
flea   The graphic phrase *He'd skin a flea for a 'aypenny* was reserved for those of a parsimonious disposition.
fleam   pocket-knife instrument used for bleeding animals. Each blade has a sharpened flag which was placed on a vein and then struck with a *bloodstick* or *mell*[1] (qv).
flecky flocker   chaffinch
Fleeakborra   Flookburgh
flick   flitch of bacon (I *flikki*)
flipe   brim of a hat (I *flipa*, a flap)
flit   to remove; *moonleet flit*

A fleam.

to strike a piece of flint in order to create a spark. With luck, the spark would then ignite the tinder, which was usually charred linen rags or dried fungus.

flouter flurry, excitement, flare

fluet sharp blow, sufficient to knock someone down

fluke, flook flat fish such as plaice, flounder or dab (see *chatterment*, *doake*, *sandscars*, *slampy*, *treading for fluke*) (OE *floc*, a flat fish)

means to move swiftly, often to avoid the *bumbailey* (qv) (I, ON *flytja*, to move; N *flyting*, removal)

Floating Island of Derwentwater Lake District equivalent of the Loch Ness Monster — believed by those who have witnessed it but dismissed by those who have not. Almost certainly the 'island' is part of the lake bed, raised to the surface in warm weather by methane and other gases. In 1815 the island measured 88 yards by 25 yards (80m by 23m), its largest recorded extent, and in 1831 it remained on the surface for more than fourteen weeks. People have picnicked on it, brass bands have played on it, and more recently a troop of Keswick Guides have planted the Union flag on it and claimed it for England! The island was last seen during the hot summer of 1995.

flodder brown scum on the water (Cartmel)

flourice iron or steel bar which was held in the knuckles and used

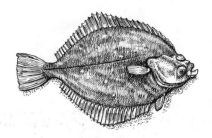

A fluke.

flummox in a stew; flustered; confused *tha's put me in a reet flummox!*

fluz'd turned up at the edges; intoxicated (see also *addled*, *in liqour*, *kalied*, *kettelt*, *tight*)

flyte to upbraid; to scold

fodderin' iron implement used for pulling hay out of a stack for fodder

fodder-gang narrow passage or gangway in front of cattle stalls in a *coo-as* (qv), by which fodder was conveyed to the animals (cf *hay-gang*) (Furness and Cartmel)

fog grass second crop of grass which follows the first mowing

foisty a musty smell or taste. Mouldy bread was usually called *foisty* (ie fusty).

folk cures Hedgerow medicine has long played an important part in Cumbrian folk life. The following remedies are known to have been used in the first half of the twentieth century:

Chest complaints: 1. smear mustard between two sheets of brown paper and tie round the chest; 2. rub with warm pit candles (used in the iron mining areas of West Cumbria and Furness)

Chapped hands: rub with warm mutton fat

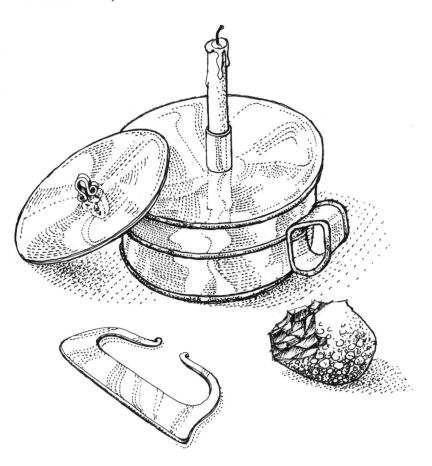

A flourice, flint, and combined tinder box, candle holder and snuffer from Townend, Troutbeck.

Boils: 1. rub with castor oil or with a bran poultice; 2. apply fresh cow dung wrapped in muslin

Stye on the eye: rub with a gold wedding ring

Stomach problem or wind in a baby: cinder tea

Chilblains: half an onion dipped in sugar and rubbed on the affected spot

Sore throats: a slice of bacon tied round the neck with a woollen sock

Spots: blackthorn flowers, brewed

(see *bacon stave*, *cinder tea*, *toothache*, *warts*, *whooping cough*, *wise men*)

foomart   pole cat; the foul martin as opposed to the pine martin (see *pine mart*)

footings   large boulders forming the foundation of a **drystone wall** (qv) (see also *cams*, *hearting*, *throughs*)

forbrest   directly in front

force   waterfall, as in Aira Force, Scale Force (I and N *foss*, waterfall)

forelders   ancestors, parents, forebears *my forelders cum fra Eshd'l* (qv) *way* (I *foreldri*, ancestor, parent)

forend   beginning *t' forend o' t' year*

fornenst   opposite to

forrat, forrad   forward, early *taties are well forrat*

forset   to obstruct, to intercept

fortree   upright bar of a gate farthest from the hinges (see *hartree*, *yat*)

fothergang   (see *fodder-gang*)

Fox and Geese   board game. A good example is to be seen in the Cowmire Hall box pew in Cartmel Fell Church. The building served as a school until 1720 and it is thought that the carving may date from that period.

Foxey   Charles Gough's faithful terrier bitch which stayed with her master for three months after his death in 1805 on Striding Edge, Helvellyn. During her vigil Foxey produced a litter of pups but they did not survive. Both Wordsworth and Scott wrote verses in praise of the steadfast dog. Scott's *Helvellyn* contains the following lines:

*How long didst thou think his
    silence was slumber?*
*When the wind wav'd his garments
    how oft didst thou start?*
*How many long days and long
    nights didst thou number*
*Ere he faded before thee the friend
    of thy heart?*

Gough was buried in the graveyard of the Quaker Meeting House at Tirril, near Penrith. Foxey was cared for by Thomas Brunskill of Crosby Garrett.

foxfire   phosphorescence on the surface of the sea (Cartmel)

foxhunting   Whatever the pros and cons, it must be admitted that foxhunting in Cumbria bears little resemblance to the colourful rituals of the shire counties. The hounds are followed on foot over the roughest country, and the devotee requires a stout pair of well-dubbined boots rather than a pink coat, a black hat and a well-groomed horse. Organised packs seem to date from the early eighteenth century — before that, foxes were trapped in whatever manner was possible (see **fox traps**). (see also *D'ye ken John Peel, hound trailing*, out-foxed, *Tally Ho! Tally Ho! Follow the Hounds*)

fox screws   fierce, vicious double 'cork' screws which, when fixed to

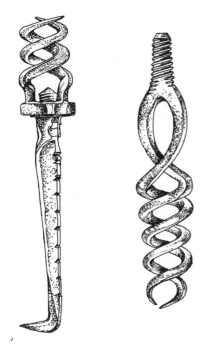

Fox screws.

a pole, were designed to extract a fox which had gone to earth in a *borran* (qv). Thankfully now illegal.

fox traps   bell-shaped corbelled drystone wall (qv) structures. Used to trap foxes in the days before

organised foxhound packs, these structures are found in the fells amongst screes and *borrans* (qv). They were baited with a dead goose, a chicken or any tasty morsel, and this was suspended from the end of a plank, like the clapper in a bell. The fox literally walked the plank to a point of no return, and was tipped into the trap, from which it could not escape because of the corbells or overhanging stones. Examples may be seen at Great Borne overlooking Ennerdale; above Levers Water, Coniston; at the Benn, Shoulthwaite Moss, Thirlmere, and several other locations.

frap   blow producing a sharp sound; to snap the finger and thumb

fratch   to argue noisily, to fall out *t' barns* (qv) *is allus fratchin'*

Frazer, Rev   long remembered for an unfinished sermon he delivered in the 1840s in Langdale Chapel. He had just taken his text, 'Behold I come quickly', when the pulpit collapsed, precipitating him suddenly onto an aged woman parishioner who, on recovering from the shock, was heard to retort: *'If I'd been kilt* [killed] *I'd been reet sarrat* [rightly served] *for ye threatened ye'd be cumming doon se'an!'*

fridge   to rub, chafe; to irritate the skin by friction

frithin month   the month immediately preceding May 13th (Old May Day) when the common pastures were kept free from stock

frosk   frog (OE *frosc*, frog)

Elaborately-constructed, drystone-walled fox traps were used in the days before organised foxhunting.

frummety barley or wheat boiled with milk

full but straight, direct *he ran at 'im full but*

full up[1] having had sufficient to eat (cf *ower-faced*)

full up[2] overcome with emotion, tearful

fultersome, fuddersom bulky, awkward

funeral biscuits made for and distributed to mourners at funerals (see *arval*)

fuz balls puffball fungus (cf *Devil's snuff box*)

G

gab¹ mouth (cf *gob*, *mun*)
gab² chat, idle talk, a great flow of words *he's got the gift of the gab*
gab³ one who gossips
gaevlock (see *gavelock*)
gaffer master, governor; a term thought to have been introduced by the first railway engineers
galivantin' in search of pleasure *she's allus galivantin' aboot*
galluses braces to hold up one's trousers
galt male pig (I *göltur*, a boar; the word is used in *Landnamabok*)
gamashers leggings, gaiters
gammerstang tall, awkward, *gaumless* (qv) person *thou gurt gammerstang!*
gammy lame, injured *Ah'm laid up* (qv) *wi' me gammy leg*
gan, gang to go
'*If thoo's gaan te gang, thoo'd best gang noo. Thoo'll hetta* [have to] *gang te platform two 'cos yon's t' train thoo wants an' thoo'd better gang, 'cos t' train's ganta gang*'
railway porter on *Peerith* (qv) Station to passengers.
gangeril, gangrill tramp, vagrant

gannan'-folk travelling people, gypsies
gap rails round poles let into stone *gate stoups* (qv)
gap stead entrance to a field closed by *gap rails* (qv)
garn yarn (I *garn*, yarn)
garrick, garrack clumsy, awkward person
garth enclosure, such as *stack-garth*, *hemp-garth* (I *garður*, an enclosure)
gate¹ thoroughfare, road; it is found in such names as Clappers-gate, Mealsgate, Sticklandgate (I, N *gata*, road, way)
gate² rights of pasturing on marshes and fells — *cattle gates*, *sheep gates*, etc
gate stoup gatepost, usually made of stone. Before *hing-ins* (qv), the *stoups* had several holes drilled into them and in these poles or *gap rails* (qv) were slotted. To allow sheep into a field, only the lowest poles needed to be removed. Some *gate stoups* bear the date when the wall was constructed.
gauk-handed left-handed
gauky, gawky awkward, ungainly

gaum gumption, shrewdness, sense; *gaumless* means without gumption *thou girt gaumless gammerstang* (qv) (cf *maezlin*) (I *gaumur*, heed, attention, consideration)

gaurdin wood used in hedging (Cartmel)

gavelock, gaevlock iron crowbar or lever (OE *gafeluc*, a lever)

gaw used in Westmorland for a young bird, but in Cartmel and Lonsdale it is used for a seagull (I *gör*, flock of gulls or crows)

gawkin, gaekan staring about in a vague manner

gawp to gape, to stare (ON *gapa*, to stare)

gay, gey, gae considerable, thoroughly *a gay bit bigger*; *there was a gay lot there*; *'I meead t' frying pan an' t' beef steeaks flee gaily murrily oot o' t'duer ...' Betty Yewdale* (qv) by A C Gibson

geal to smart, to itch, to ache with cold

gebby, yebby crook-handled stick; knob-stick; cudgel

gedderen' spot meeting place

geldert, gildert snare made of horse hair used for catching small birds (see also *sprint*) (ON *gilder*, a snare; I *gildra*, a trap)

gerawaback, gerawaby orders to a sheepdog to go further out and to bring the sheep in

Gersma Grasmere

get it, git it retribution, punishment *wait till thy fadder* (qv) *gits yam* (qv) — *tha'll git it!*

gettin' on growing older *Ike must be gettin' on now*

gezzlins goslings (see also *May gezzlin*) (I *gaeslingur*, goslings)

A gavelock or gaevlock.

Giant's Grave group of two ancient stone crosses and four 'hogback' tombstones standing in St Andrew's churchyard, Penrith. Legend says that here lies Sir Eweine Caesarious, a famous warrior, but when the stones were re-set in 1888, only a few fragments of human bones were found. Close by is a single cross known as the Giant's Thumb. The stones are probably 1,000 years old.

gift-again the small amount of money given back 'for luck' on settling a bargain (cf *luck penny*)

Gilcruise Gilcrux

gill ravine; in the nineteenth century the spelling 'ghyll' became common, eg Dungeon Ghyll (ON *gill*, a ravine, deep gully)

gimmer female sheep that has not yet borne a lamb (I, N *gimbr*, a female yearling sheep)

ginnel narrow passage between two buildings

An iron girdle plate used in the making of haver bread.

The Giant's Grave, Penrith.

girdle plate iron plate used for baking *haver bread* (qv). In the north of Cumbria the term becomes *griddle*.

girn (see *gurn*)

girt great, large; *Girt Langden* is Great Langdale

Girt Saffel Great Salkeld

giss-giss-giss the call to young pigs (cf *yuly-yuly*); *he nowther said giss ner sty* means he said nothing (see *gris*)

give o'er desist from, refrain from, stop. An exasperated mother will frequently say to a *greetin'* (qv) *child*: *'Give o'er gurnin'* (qv) *!'*

giversum avaricious, greedy

gizzern, gizzin gizzard; *it fair sticks in me gizzern* means that something is remembered with unpleasant feelings

glead   kite (hawk)

gleean   squinting

glee-eyed   cross-eyed (north Cumbria)

gliff   brief look, glimpse *Ah just gat a gliff o' it*

glime   a glance aside; to look askance at something

glisky   bright, sparkling; when said of the weather, *ower glisky* means 'Too bright too early'! (ON *glyssa*, sparkle)

gloppened   astonished, amazed *Ah was fair gloppened!* (I *glupnaðr*, ON *glupna*, astonished)

gloppers   blinkers for a horse

glower, gloor   to stare with wide eyes

glumpen   to look surly

glunch   to look angry

go bye   get away; instruction given to a sheepdog

gob   mouth (see *gab*, *mun*)

gob-stopper   large spherical sweet which changed colour as it was sucked

godspeed   wooden screen within a door

gollin   marsh marigold

gollop   to eat greedily and hastily *tha mun't* (qv) *gollop thi poddish* (qv) *!* (cf *wulf*)

gomeral, gomaral   braggart, bully, cowardly fellow (I *gambra*, to boast)

good an' all   entirely, finally *Aye, he's gone for good an' all*

good tails   good catch of fish (Cartmel)

goose bow   bow hung around the neck of a goose to prevent it from getting through hedges

The Fishing Stone, Gosforth — the ultimate in fishermen's tales.

goosegogs, goosegobs   gooseberries. A children's expression used in the centre and south of Cumbria; in the north, the term gooseberry is common (cf *berries*, *grossers*)

Gosforth Cross   Arguably the finest Anglo-Scandinavian cross in England, this slender fourteen and a half foot (4.4m) high sandstone

Gosforth Fishing Stone

Gosforth Warrior's Tomb

cross shaft has stood on the same spot in Gosforth churchyard for almost 1,000 years. Carved by people of Norse-Irish extraction, it shows, on the east side, the Crucifixion, but on the other three sides there are representations of the Norse pagan gods such as Loki, Heimdal and Vidar, as well as fierce dragons and serpents so often found in Norse mythology. It has been interpreted as representing Ragnarok, the overthrow of the old gods, and the triumph of the White Christ, and the emergence of a new religion. (see 'Bound Devil', Gosforth Fishing Stone)

of the god Thor fishing for the World Serpent. Thor is identified by his hammer held in his right hand; in his left he holds his fishing line, at the end of which is the bait — the head of an ox. His companion, the giant Hymir, terrified of the World Serpent, holds an axe and is about to cut the line and allow the monster to go free. Undoubtedly this must be the ultimate in fishermen's tales! Stones illustrating the same story may be seen in Denmark and Sweden. (see 'Bound Devil', Gosforth Cross)

Gosforth Saint's Tomb one of two hogback tombstones at the

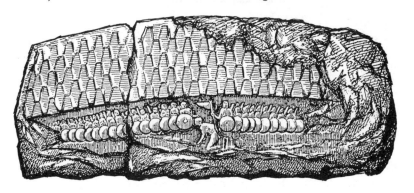

The Warrior's hogback tomb, Gosforth.

Gosforth Fishing Stone discovered in 1882 during alterations to the church. Perhaps part of a frieze, the upper part of the stone seems to represent a hart trampling on a serpent or snake, while the lower portion illustrates a story — well-known throughout the whole of Scandinavian world —

west end of Gosforth Church (see **Gosforth Warrior's Tomb**). The name is fanciful and probably derives from a representation of the Crucifixion carved on one end of the tombstone.

Gosforth Warrior's Tomb the second of two Viking hogback tombstones in Gosforth Church.

The Saint's Tomb, Gosforth.

On one side, two armies, equipped with round shields and weapons, may be seen facing each other. Does it commemorate a great battle? (see **Gosforth Saint's Tomb**)

Gough, John (1757–1825) the Kendal polymath, was blinded by smallpox in early childhood but excelled in the Quaker school in Kendal, and later was revered as an outstanding teacher of mathematics, botany, geology, physics and zoology. Among his pupils was **John Dalton** (qv). Coleridge admired him greatly and **Wordsworth** (qv) lionises him in *The Excursion.* (see *dales larnin'*)

gowk[1] cuckoo (I, ON *gaukur*, cuckoo)

gowk[2] fool; in the north of the county, *April gowk* means April Fool (see *Borrowdale gowk*)

gowlan crying, sobbing

gowpen, gowpin as much as two hands will hold together (I *gaupn*, two hands held together to form a bowl)

gradely genuine, excellent, readily *t' rain cum down in a gradely girt pelt* (qv) (much used in Lancashire)

grand splendid, excellent *it wer a reet grand do*

granny-wittles small, sharp ridges on the sand (Cartmel)

graphite (see *wad*)

grapplin' common method of catching trout by wading in the becks and grappling the fish by hand from under stones or in holes

Grasmere dialect plays series of plays written by Grasmere people largely for their own entertainment. They were originally presented at the end of January or in the first half of February.

The first play, *The Dalesman*, was written in 1893 by Miss Charlotte Fletcher, the daughter of the Rector of Grasmere, but subsequently they were written by Miss Eleanor Simpson (Mrs H D **Rawnsley**(qv)). All profits were given to local charities.

Grasmere gingerbread originally *rushbearers' gingerbread* and was given as a reward for strewing rushes on the church floor (see *rushbearing*). This biscuit-like gingerbread is still baked in a small building, formerly the village school, in the corner of the churchyard.

Grasmere Sports always held on the third Thursday in August, Grasmere Sports is one of the most important fixtures in the Lakeland sporting calendar. Originally held in a field behind the Red Lion Inn after the annual *rushbearing* (qv), the sports were later moved to the present site east of the village, and here thousands of people gather to watch **wrestling** (qv), *hound trailing* (qv), sprinting, and, for many people the great event of the day, the gruelling Guides' Race to the summit of Butter Crag and back. (see *blaan oot*)

grass nail small iron hook connecting the scythe blade with the shaft

grave to dig, especially peats; in the north-east of Cumbria *delve* is also common (I *grafa*, OE *grafan*, to dig)

Graysoon Graysouthen

green-Christmas mild early winter; *a green-Christmas maks a fat kirk-yard* reflects the fear that a mild spell in November and December would later lead to ill-health

greenhew rent paid by the tenants of the Manor of Plain Furness for the right to cut timber in Sowerby and other manorial woods. It was introduced in the time of Queen Elizabeth I.

grees *horsin' stone* (qv) or mounting block (south Cumbria)

greetin' weeping, whimpering *gi' o'er greetin'!*

grey peats (see *peat pot*)

greymin, grimin thin covering or spotting of snow (cf *daad*)

Greystick Greystoke

griddle (see *girdle*)

gripe large stable fork used for moving manure (cf *muck hack*)

gris, grise swine, young pigs; the word appears in several place names such as Grizedale and Grizebeck (see *giss-giss-giss*) (I *gris*, D *gris*, a young pig)

grizzlin' (see *greetin'*)

groaning cheese eaten to celebrate the birth of a child. William Fleming records in his diary in 1818:

... as soon as the good woman was delivered ... the accoucher [male midwife] cut a slice or two of the cheese, then cross-cut them into pieces about the size of a finger and shook them in his shirt lap; these were distributed among the unmarried women to lay under their pillows at night to dream of. This cheese is called the Groaning Cheese of which all present ate heartily and drank the

'Gurning through a braffin' is a traditional Cumbrian pastime.

warm ale mixed with rum or brandy after which the married woman leapt over a besom (qv) or birch broom and she who did not clear the broom was pronounced the next for the straw

grossers gooseberries (cf **berries**, **goosegogs**) (north-east Cumbria)

grundlin ringed plover

gumption similar to **gaum** (qv)

Gunpowder Plot The 1605 plot is commemorated by a set of Latin hexameters painted on an arch in the interior of St Martin's Church, Bowness-on-Windermere. Legend says they were written by Christopher Philipson of Calgarth Hall in 1629. In translation the inscription reads:

This is a day more famed as each year brings it round. Rejoice, good men. The mischief conspired in Stygian gloom has been made an empty tale by the hand of Providence. England, which was to be conspicuous by the greatness of its ruin, may now sing hymns, since she has remained free by the grace of Heaven

gurn, girn literally, to grin. ***Girnin' through a braffin*** (qv) is a Cumbrian pastime — the winner is judged to be the person who makes the most grotesque face — with or without dentures! Peevish children are often **bidden** (qv) by their mothers to ***stop thi gurnin'***. (see **Egremont Crab Fair**)

H

haaf net net with a *poke[1]* (qv), used in sea fishing, especially on the Solway coasts (I *haf*, the sea)

hack pudding large dumpling eaten at sheep *clippings* (qv)

hacks (see *kinns*)

hag[1] to cut or chop with an axe

hag[2] woody place intermixed with grass

hag berry, heck berry bird cherry; Wordsworth called it 'cluster-cherry'. It is often mistaken for lilac.

hag-clog, hag-stock chopping block

hag worm common snake or adder. The term is common throughout much of Cumbria, but in the north-east the word *ether* is used, and in parts of Westmorland, 'adder' is common. (I *högg-ormur*, snake or serpent)

hagger one who cuts coal at the coalface

hak pick axe

hake riotous festivity; tumult (see *Auld Wives' Hake, merry neet*)

hallan passage from the front to the back of a farmhouse, separating the service area (see *down house*) from the living accommodation (see *fire house*)

hallan drop black, sooty liquid which fell down the open chimneys in wet weather, often onto the heads of those seated below. Arguably the reason why dalesmen still keep their caps on indoors.

Hallowe'en the Eve of All Saints' Day, the 31st October (see *Hanchin' Neet, Duck Apple Night*)

halts (see *holts*)

hammer-bleat, heather-bleat snipe; in the breeding season the call of the male birds resembles the bleating of a goat

ham-samm irregular; all in confusion

hand-fastened bargain or agreement sealed only by the striking of hands

handsel, hansel bargain, generally applied to the money that crosses the hand from the first bargain (I *handsöl*, the transference of a right, bargain or duty to another by the shaking of hands; ON *handsala*, a bargain)

handsturn work, occupation *he nivver did a handsturn in his life*

hankering the heel move in Cumberland and Westmorland

Hanshin' Neet, or Hallowe'en.

wrestling (qv) in which the attacker twines his left leg around his opponent's right leg

hankle to entangle, to knot (I *hanka*, to fasten, to knot)

hansel (see *handsel*)

hansh, hanch to snap the jaws (see *hanshin' neet*)

Hanshin' Neet Hallowe'en. A traditional pastime was *hanshin'* for apples hung from a string —

the competitors' hands being tied behind their backs. (see **bobbing the apple**, **Duck Apple Night**)

hap to wrap, to cover *hap yersel well up*

happen perhaps *happen he's lost his way* (cf *mappen*)

happen on to come across, to encounter *Ah just happened on 't by luck*

happins thick woollen bed covers

Sir Edward de Harcla, identified by his shield, defends Carlisle Castle against the Scots in 1315.

happy as a pig in muck contented

Harcla, Sir Edward de (?–1323) loyal defender of Carlisle against the besieging Scots in 1315, for which action he was made Earl of Carlisle. However, in 1322 he lost favour and was accused by Edward II of negotiating a peace treaty with Robert Bruce. Condemned as a traitor, he was hanged at Harraby, outside Carlisle, his head was sent to London and other parts of his body were despatched to Carlisle, Newcastle and elsewhere. Ironically, Edward was forced to make a truce with the Scots in the same year.

hard agin close to *t' lathe's* (qv) *hard agin yon rowan* (qv)

hardbacks cockles; to go *hardbacking* is to go cockling (Cartmel) (see also *coul, cramb, jumbo, skeear, teanal, wheaat*)

harden rough material used for coarse aprons or *brats* (qv). A *harden sark* was a shirt made from this material which had to be washed several times and beaten with a *battlin' stick* (qv) on a *battlin' steean* (qv) before it could be worn. (see *sark*)

Hard Wark Nivver Kilt Anybody ancient old wives' tale elegantly refuted by an ostentatious gravestone in Rampside churchyard, Low Furness. John Dickinson died in January 1878, aged forty-one years; his grieving mother blamed her daughter-in-law for her son's untimely demise, as the inscription clearly shows:

Here lies my tortured son
For comfort of late he had none

But the most crushing indictment appears at the base of the memorial:

It was 232 hours labour in 12 days
That brought poor John to his
    grave

harpin' on to constantly refer to an unpleasant happening *stop thi harpin' on*

hartree upright bar of a gate next to the hinges (see *fortree, yat*)

hask cold, dry weather

has ta? hes ta? have you?

hasty pudding form of porridge made with oatmeal and water, and eaten with butter and treacle. William Dickinson, writing of Westmorland in 1852, claimed that 'a great quantity of oats is ground into meal and made into porridge and this, with milk, bread and sometimes cheese, constitutes the breakfast and the supper of the chief part of the farm households in the county'. Alternatively, oatmeal was made into *crowdy* (qv), a form of soup in which the stock from boiling meat was poured over the meal. (see *poddish*)

haver oats (I *hafrar*, oats)

haver bread thin, unleaven oat bread which would keep for many months (cf *clapbread, oatbread*)

hawthorn Sometimes called *white thorn* or *May tree*, it was associated with places of trial or areas where justice was delivered. The bringing of hawthorn blossom into houses was thought to bring ill-luck or even death. (see also *bread and cheese*)

hay-gang gangway leading from

the barn or hayloft to the cow-stalls (cf *fodder-gang*)

heaf the portion of the fell attached to each fell farm as sheep pasture; a sheep walk. *Heaf gang-an* or *hefted* sheep are animals which are let along with the farm and pastured on a particular *heaf*.

hearth cults The hearth was the focal point of all Cumbrian farmhouses and, around the glow of a peat fire, the traditions and the folk stories were transmitted from one generation to the next. There was a strong belief that the fire should never be allowed to go out, otherwise ill-fortune would befall the family; consequently, fires were carefully tended, even in the warmest of summers. H S Cowper, writing in 1897, recorded that the fires at Lawson Park and Parkamoor, two remote farms high above Coniston Water, had not been extinguished for centuries. Of course, there could be another reason for the maintenance of the fire — the difficulty of re-lighting it using a flint and a *flourice* (qv).

heartings small stones used as filling in **drystone walls** (qv) (see also *cams*, *footings*, *throughs*)

heck¹, eck moveable tailboard of a two-wheeled wooden farm cart (cf *end board*, *skut¹*)

heck² partition forming the passage connecting the *hallan* (qv) with the *fire house* (qv) (cf *mell passage*)

heck berry (see *hag berry*)

Helm wind very fierce, cold, easterly wind which blows down from Cross Fell into the Eden Valley. The appearance of a lenticular (lens-shaped) cloud over the fell is regarded as a sure sign that the Helm is about to descend. A modified version can be experienced in Grasmere, Rydal and Keswick when similar clouds form on Fairfield and Skiddaw. Wordsworth observed the effects on the 30th March 1822, and recorded that 'the winds have been acting on the small Lake of Rydal, as if they had received command to carry its waters from their bed to the sky ... Frequently an eddying wind scooped the waters out of the basin, and forced them upwards in the very shape of an Icelandic geysir or boiling fountain, to the height of several hundred feet.'

Helvellyn once thought to be one of the highest mountains in England, giving rise to the old rhyme:

Skiddaw, Lauvellin [sic] *and Casticam* [sic]
Are the highest hills climbed by Englishmen

It is certainly one of the most visited summits in the Lake District, barely a day passing without someone standing at its cairn. **Dr John Dalton** (qv) climbed to its summit on at least forty occasions to measure the dew point. Today it is reached by mountain bikes and even motorcycles; in 1926 an Avro Alpha aeroplane made a landing (and took off again after the pilot had asked for directions!) And of course it is the 'sunrise mountain', visited by many hill-walkers wishing to see the first rays of a new day. It also has more memorials than any other

Cumbrian mountain: one, built in 1890, is located above the spot where Charles Gough died (see **Foxey**); another, on Striding Edge, commemorating Mr Dixon, a fox-hunting man, was placed there in 1858, and a third near the summit marks the spot where the aircraft landed.

hemplin hedge sparrow

hen-pen hen-bane

hen-pennies small, pink bivalve shellfish (Cartmel)

henscrats, henscarts cirrus cloud

hen silver money begged at the church door after a wedding ceremony (see *shellin' out, sneckin' up t' yat*)

herb pudding (see *Easterledge pudding*)

Herdwick sheep The term *Herdwick* was first used by the Cistercian monks of Furness Abbey to indicate a sheep farm, but it later became identified with the specific breed of sheep. Despite legends which claim that the original animals were washed ashore from wrecks of Viking ships or even Armada vessels, the breed probably originates from animals bred in the Bronze Age. *Herdwicks* will withstand harsh conditions better than any other breed and can survive burial under snow for many days. They have white faces and legs, though the lambs for the first year are brown-black. Their wool is coarse and *full o' kemps* (qv), but when properly cooked the mutton is fit for a queen (see *tatie-pot*). (see also *mugg*, *Teeswatter*, *Swaddle*)

hermits Cumbria seems to have attracted more than its fair share of hermits. As well as **St Herbert** (qv), one of the best known was George Smith (c1825–1876), who was known as the **Skiddaw Hermit** or the **Dodd Man** because he lived in a 'nest' on Skiddaw Dodd. Inordinately fond of whisky, he made a living of sorts by painting portraits and dabbling in phrenology. Ejected from Keswick by the local constabulary, he lived for a time on the shores of Windermere in a small tent. Eventually, having given up drink, he returned to his native Aberdeenshire where he died. **Millican Dalton** (1867–1947) styled himself 'Professor of Adventure'; although teetotal, he was addicted to coffee and Woodbine cigarettes! He lived in a cave on Castle Crag in Borrowdale and eked out an existence

A Herdwick tup.

Millican Dalton, 'Professor of Adventure', lived as a hermit in a cave in Borrowdale.

by guiding and teaching rock-climbing. His obituary included the words 'A man of simple pleasures and tastes ... a mind at peace with the world', and over the entrance to his cave he carved the enigmatic legend 'Don't!! Waste Words. Jump to Conclusions'.

hesp door *sneck* (qv) (I *hespa*, catch for a door)

high cockalorum (see *monti-kitty*)

hinberry, hineberry raspberry

hinderends (see *inderends*)

hingan' his lugs literally, hanging his ears — crestfallen

hing-ins hinges of a gate (see also *jimmer*, *stangers*, *yat*) (south Cumbria)

hingin' in t' bell ropes period during which wedding banns are read in church

hipe (see *hype*)

hipping baby's napkin

Hird, Hugh Often called the 'Troutbeck Giant', the legendary Hugh Hird is said to have visited London sometime in the fifteenth or sixteenth century — the dates are vague — and defeated the king's champion in a wrestling bout. On being asked about his diet, Hird is supposed to have said that he ate *'thick poddish that a mouse might walk on dry-shod for breakfast and the sunny side of a wether* [sheep] *for dinner'*. A good **Will Ritson**-like (qv) story — but apocryphal.

hiring fairs Hiring fairs were held at Whitsun and Martinmas, the most important being those at Cockermouth, Carlisle, Kendal, Keswick, Penrith and Ulverston. Farm servants not **stopping on** (qv) for a further six months, stood in the market place with a straw **brobb** (qv) in their hats or their mouths, indicating that they were for hire. On completion of negotiations, the master gave the newly-hired servant **arles** (qv) or **earnest money**, usually a shilling, as a token of their agreement. Hirings continued until the Second World War, lingering on in Carlisle until the early 1950s. (see **arles**, **festing penny**, **runnigate**, **toothpullers**, **warts**)

hirplen aboot walking with difficulty because of lameness or infirmity (cf **hitchen**)

hisk to gasp for breath (I *hiksta*, to sob, to hiccup)

hissel himself

hista! hurry up!, make haste!

hitch steppin' hop, step and *loup* (qv). Now an Olympic event...

hitchen (see *hirplen*)

hobthrush, hob A hobgoblin or spirit which will do much useful work about the farm if left to itself but if crossed or coaxed in any way it is liable to do mischief. Sometimes known as *Robin Good-fellow*.

hocker[1] to crouch over the fire

hocker[2] one who sits at home

hod on! stop! wait a minute! (OE *healdan*, wait)

hodden grey Sometimes known as *self-grey* or *Skiddaw-grey*, this grey woollen cloth was woven from yarn spun from white wool and black wool. This was the origin of John Peel's 'coat so grey'.

Hoggart, Thomas Tom Hoggart (1642–1709) was the village carpenter in Troutbeck (Westmorland) in the second half of the seventeenth century. In addition to his woodworking skills, he enjoyed a reputation as a writer of *play-jiggs*, short plays in rhyme written for the village players. His best known works are *The Lascivious Queen*, performed in the open air in 1693, and *The Destruction of Troy*, for which he built an enormous wooden horse from which men emerged at the critical moment. Clearly, this untutored Cumbrian carpenter had the panache of a Cecil B DeMille. He also had a penchant for writing epitaphs, of which the best known is 'For a Woman':

Here lies a woman,
No man can deny it,
She died in peace, though she
    lived unquiet;
Her husband prays if e'er this way
    you walk,
You would tread softly — if she
    wake she'll talk

hoggas, hoggast, hogus sheep shelter for wintering lambs after weaning

hoggs, hogs, hoggets yearling sheep (see *hoggas, hogg-holes*)

hogg-holes holes made in the base of **drystone walls** (qv) to allow sheep to pass from one pasture to another. If only one section of the pasture is required, the *hogg-hole* is blocked with a stone or *flag* (qv).

hogg-squarl period of stormy weather in April, which coincides with the time the *hoggs* go onto the fells

Holker or Hoaker? which pronunciation? Lord Cavendish of Furness, who resides at Holker Hall in Cartmel, insists on 'Hoaker', but the vast majority of Barrow residents are equally firm that their soccer team plays at the Ho*L*ker Street ground. BBC Radio Cumbria, meanwhile, sits on the fence and uses 'Hoaker' for the hall and Ho*L*ker for the football ground.

holy-stones (see *dobby stones*)

holy wells and spas Cumbria has a surprising number of medicinal wells. The Romans were aware of the healing properties of the Gilsland spring, but the spa did not develop fully until the eighteenth and nineteenth centuries. The Borrowdale salt spring

Hogg-holes allow sheep to move between pastures separated by drystone walls.

at Manesty was used in the eighteenth century, while the Stanger Spa in the Vale of Lorton and Gutterby Spa on the south-west Cumbrian coast were popular in the nineteenth century. The Holy Well at Humphrey Head in Cartmel, once the property of Cartmel Priory, was well-known in the seventeenth century, and was visited by leadminers from the Alston area who claimed it cured them of various occupational ailments. In the twentieth century, bottled water from the well was sold on Morecambe promenade, pre-dating supermarket brands by ninety years! The well at Witherslack was credited with miraculous powers such as the eradication of leprosy and worms. The last serious attempt to establish a spa was at Shap Wells, where the hotel dates from 1848.

hollin holly. Much prized and harvested in the eighteenth century as winter fodder for sheep — the resulting mutton having a particularly fine flavour. The practise continued in Great Langdale and elsewhere until the 1920s.

holts, halts, hots wicker pannier baskets on each side of a horse, used for transporting peats, *elding* (qv) etc (cf *muck hots*)

hood neuk area under the chimney hood and close to the fire. The warmest, cosiest place in the farmhouse on a wet winter's night, despite the main disadvantage of *hallan drop* (qv).

Horn of the Hunter well-known hunting song, usually heard at hunt suppers

horning administering of liquid medicine to an animal. Traditionally, the dose was mixed in a large cow's horn and then poured into the animal's throat.

horse knop knapweed

horse stang dragonfly (cf *bull stang*) (Furness)

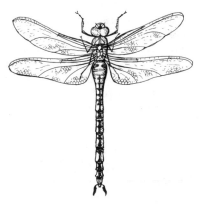

A horse stang.

horsin' stone mounting block or steps from which horses were mounted (cf *grees*)

hos, hoss horse. An epitaph on a Kendal gravestone reads:
Here lies John Ross
Kicked by a hoss

hound trailing sometimes called 'the poor man's **foxhunting** (qv)'. Rarely seen outside the area, the sport has become one of the most popular in Cumbria. The hounds follow a trail laid by rags soaked in aniseed and oil over fell and dale, mountain and moorland for eight or nine miles. The hounds are not foxhounds and the two must not be confused; trail hounds are bred for speed and can achieve twenty miles an hour (30kph) in the pursuit of the aniseed trail. The sight — and sound — of a group of excited owners breaking into a cacophony of yells, screams, and whistles to encourage their hounds to the finishing line has to be experienced to be believed.

house   (see *fire house*)

house leek traditionally grown on the outside of buildings to protect against lightning strikes. It was also believed that **warts** (qv) could be removed by rubbing with the fleshy leaves of this plant.

howdy, houdy-wife midwife (see *accouchers*)

howk to pull up by the roots, to excavate, to scoop out

hubbleshoo commotion *there was such a hubbleshoo*

hull shed or shelter such as *rabbit hull*, *pig hull*, *hen hull* etc

hullet, youlet owl

humming grog (see *powsowdy*)

hunkers haunches

hunting nuts small, round gingerbreads, traditionally made in Cartmel. They were small enough to be carried in the pockets when going hunting.

hurkel, hocker to crouch, to stoop, to huddle together (I *hokra*, ON *hurka*, to crouch)

A hullet.

hurries wooden chutes through which coal was loaded directly into the holds of sailing ships in Whitehaven harbour. Horse-drawn wagons brought the coal from the pit to a point above the chutes, then a lever was used to release the hinged bottom of the wagon, allowing the coal to be shot into the ship below.

hype, hipe to throw over the hip in Cumberland and Westmorland **wrestling** (qv). Varieties include *swinging hype* and *standing hype*.

I

ill¹ to degrade or slander *don't ill a body if you can't say well o' yan*

ill² evil *he's been an ill ket-kite* (qv) *o' his life* (I *illur*, bad, evil, ill)

ill-set to find difficulty in accomplishing something *Ah's ill-set to mek a living*

ill thing sick person *she looked like an ill thing, poor soul*

ill-tongues revilers, detractors

ill-turn an injury, a wrong

in-anunder underneath

inbank, inhill down hill

inbye land good quality pasture surrounding the farmstead, as opposed to *intak land* (qv)

'inderends small, withered grain, used as a feed for poultry; light grain blown out of the *hinder end* of the winnowing machine

infield (see *inbye land*)

ing meadows, cow pastures (N *ing*, a field, meadow)

inkle coarse, narrow tapes; *thick as inkle weavers* means very intimate

inklin' slight hint or intimation *she had no inklin' o' it*

insense to make one understand *Ah can't insense it intil* (qv) *him*

in liquor euphemism for being drunk (cf *addled, fluz'd, kalied, kettelt, tight*)

intak land land which has been enclosed or taken in from the fell or common (cf *inbye land*)

intil into

iron boat Tradition says that the first iron boat in the world was made at an iron furnace at Wilson House in Cartmel around 1750. 'Iron-mad' **John Wilkinson** (qv) is believed to have constructed a shallow-draught iron vessel to bring peat down the River Winster to fuel his furnace at Wilson House. In the 1870s there were people alive who claimed to have seen the boat in the early decades of that century, and there are those in Cartmel who believe that it still exists, buried in the mud of Helton Tarn. A project for the National Maritme Museum, perhaps?

ishokles icicles (N *isjökel*, icicle)

ista? are you? *Ista gaan til Peerith* (qv) *?*

ist'er? is there ? *Ist'er any poddish* (qv) *left?*

iversome always

J

jack *black powder* (qv) or gunpowder; slate-quarrying term

jacket and waistcoat fleece good-quality fleece

jaggin cartful

jammy crane heron

janglement angry disputation

jannock, jannak fair, honest, straightforward, even *it's not jannock*

jarble to splash with mud

jedder to rattle, to vibrate with a quick rattling noise as windows in

A jammy crane.

a strong wind or teeth with cold

jenny hole ventilation hole in the gable end of a barn; sometimes called the *owl hole* (qv) since it is used by owls when hunting vermin

jenny red tail common redstart

Jew Stone In Mallerstang, close to the Cumbria-Yorkshire border, is arguably one of the most unusual monuments in the North of England. The original limestone column was set up in Black Fell Moss, below Hugh's Seat (see **Moreville, Sir Hugh de**) by William Mounsey, a member of a famous Rockcliffe family. Mounsey was a strange, mystic figure who, after military service in the Middle East, developed a long and lasting affection for the Jewish faith and culture. In 1850 he made a pilgrimage on foot from the Solway to the source of the River Eden. On reaching his journey's end, he built a monument to commemorate the event; this bore the Star of David, texts in Latin and Greek, and a back-to-front latinised version of his name – YESNUOM SUMLEILUG. Unfortunately the stone was shattered in 1870 by a group of Settle-Carlisle Railway navvies who did not share Mounsey's classical education. For many years the fragments lay on the fellside, but ultimately they ended up in a barn in Mallerstang awaiting restoration. Although this was not possible, a group of enthusiasts in Britain and in Israel raised sufficient funds for a facsimile to be erected on Outhgill village green, and this was unveiled on the 21st September 1989.

jike, jeyk to creek or squeak, like an axle needing greasing or new shoes when first worn

jiking rasping cough (Cartmel)

jigger one who is skilled in dancing

jiggered tired out, exhausted *Ah'm fair jiggered!* (cf *paggered*)

jimmer, jemmer butt hinges of a door (see *hing-ins*)

jinny green teeth green algae on ponds

jinny spinners sycamore seeds (cf *pigeon flyers*)

jip pain, discomfort *toothwark's givin' me jip*

job nuts cob nuts

joggly rough, uneven *it's nobbut a joggly road*

Johnson, David well-known nineteenth century 'character' and driver of a local mailcoach. In 1840 he was involved in an early example of 'road rage'. **William Wordsworth** (qv) and his son John were travelling in a one-horse gig; two or three miles outside Keswick they were struck by Johnson's mail coach, which flung the two Wordsworths, the horse, the gig and part

of a drystone wall into a field. Years later, David Johnson related the tale of how he had *'spilt the Wadsworths'* (sic) and confessed that he had *'nivver heard a body's tongue sweer* [swear] *gladlier, though, for I thowt we'd kilt t' poit'*.

Jolly Boys (see *pace egg song*)

Jones, John Paul (1747–1792) born at Kirkbean in Kirkudbrightshire. He was apprenticed to a Whitehaven merchant and later became third mate on the *King George*, a slaving vessel sailing out of Whitehaven to West Africa and the American colonies. On the outbreak of the War of Independence, Jones applied for and received a commission in the fledgling Congressional Navy, and in 1777 was given command of the *Ranger*. On the night of the 22nd–23rd April 1778, the *Ranger* mounted a daring attack on Whitehaven, spiking thirty-six cannon in the Half Moon battery and setting fire to a coal ship, the *Thompson*, in the harbour. The raid resulted in minimal material damage, but the effect on morale was considerable, for Jones had tweaked the lion's tail and the government in London was not pleased. Jones later became a rear-admiral in the navy of Catherine the Great, and died in Paris in 1792. In 1913 his remains were removed to the US Naval Academy in Annapolis.

jope, joap to splash, to bespatter

joss to jostle, to tease

jossen crowded, squeezed

jumbo wooden boards on two

The 'jumbo' (foreground) and the 'cramb' are used in the gathering of cockles in Morecambe Bay.

long handles used to activate the sands to bring cockles to the surface. Probably so named about a hundred years ago because of its size. (see also *coul, cramb, hardbacks, skeear, teanal, wheaat*)

jumper　pointed iron bar used by quarrymen to drill the hole for the ***black powder*** (qv). The bar was struck with a hammer, turned, then hit once more, and so on. A hole about six feet (2m) deep was considered a good day's work.

juniper　(see *savin*)

K

kaikin', kaykin' to wander about stupidly *kaykin' about like a pet goose*

kak-handed left-handed

kale pot Sometimes known as a *pot oven*, this versatile household utensil was a cast-iron pan with a lid, which sat on the fire on three small legs to allow the fire to burn under it. Completely covered with burning peat, it could be used as an oven to bake cakes and pies, but if suspended over the fire from a *rattencrook* (qv), it would serve as a hash or stew pan.

kali (pron *kay-lie*) sherbet powder

kalied slang expression meaning intoxicated *he's kalied again* (cf *addled, fluz'd, in liquor, kettelt, tight*)

kaykin' (see *kaikin'*)

kebby stick walking stick

keck to tip up a cart, to unload

kecks trousers

keckley, cockley unsteady, easily upset

keds sheep lice and parasites

keek to peep

keep food, sustenance *Ah was workin' fer nowt but ma keep an' a laal bit bacca*

keish cow parsnip; water hemlock. Boys used the stems to make pop-guns.

keld well or spring; found in place names such as Keld, near Shap, and Brotherilkeld in Eskdale (I, ON *kelda*, a spring)

kelp (see *tangel*)

kelter, kilter order, condition; *out of kelter* means in poor condition

kelterment, kelderment odds and ends, bits and pieces

kemps hairs amongst the wool of a fleece, giving it a coarse quality

ken to know, to recognise *'D' ye ken John Peel?'* (I *kenna*, to know)

Kendal bowmen (see *archery*)

Kendal green green cloth which made Kendal famous throughout England. Falstaff in *Henry IV Part 1* speaks of the 'three misbegotten knaves in Kendal green' who attacked him, but there is an earlier reference in 1497 to 'greene Kentdales'. The cloth was first dyed yellow using an extract from dyers' greenweed (*Genista tinctoria*), then it was re-dyed using a blue dye, probably made from woad but later using indigo.

Kendal Mint Cake If you search through the iron rations of polar explorers, lone round-the-world yachtspersons, long-distance walkers, and Himalayan and Alpine mountaineers, inevitably you will find that high-energy glucose confection, **Kendal Mint Cake**. Thought to have been developed by accident in 1868 when Joseph Wiper was boiling sugar in his sweet shop, the event proved fortunate for the Wiper family and for Kendal. Sir Ernest Shackleton took **KMC** to Antarctica, and Sir Edmund Hillary records how, in 1953 on the roof of the world, he and Tenzing 'sat on the snow and looked at the country far below us … we nibbled Kendal Mint Cake'. Today **KMC** comes in brown, white and chocolate-covered — and even a variety endorsed by **Wainwright** (qv)!

Kendal wiggs (see *whiggs*)

kenspecked, kenspeckl't branded, marked, conspicuous

kent-faced well-known face

keowl small piece of wood or bone which was used to measure the mesh when making fishing nets (south Cumbria) (I *kefla*, a round stick, roller or horse-gag)

kep to catch while falling; to fish with a hook and line. *Kepping/kebbing* is still used for fishing with hooks and lines in Walney Channel and Morecambe Bay. (I *kippa*, to pull, wrench, to pick)

keps fishing tackle consisting of a lead weight and two curved wires, from the end of which dangle strings and hooks and bait

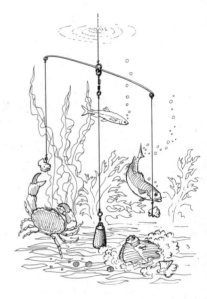

Keps are used when 'kepping' or 'kebbing' for fish in Morecambe Bay.

kern supper *merry neet* (qv) to celebrate the end of the harvest (cf *mell supper*) (?from 'corn')

Kersmas Christmas

Kersmas sheaf sheaf of corn given to each cow or horse on Christmas morning (see *mell²*)

Keskadale oaks small group of sessile oak trees at a height of 1,000–1,400 feet (300–425m) above sea level, in Keskadale in the Derwent Fells. Some authorities believe that these trees are survivors of the native oak forest which once covered most of Cumbria's hills and mountains.

keslop rennet; calf's fourth stomach used for curdling milk (I *kaesir*, rennet, and *hlaup*, coagulated milk)

kessen discarded, cast off; a *kessened sheep* is one which is lying on its back, unable to get up; *kessened o'er* is also used for a cloudy sky

Keswick codlin type of apple introduced by John Saunders, a Keswick nurseryman, at the end of the eighteenth century

ket carrion, offal, filth (I *ket*, *kjöt*, flesh)

ket craw carrion crow

ket-kite derogatory term indicating a person of mean actions

ketlock wild mustard

ketmar the tern

kettelt kettled, ie under the influence of alcohol (cf *addled*, *fluz'd*, *in liquor*, *kalied*, *tight*)

keys childrens' truce word (cf *skinch*)

kicking donkey (see *montikitty*)

kile, kyle boil, abscess (I *kyli*, a boil, an abscess)

kilter (see *kelter*)

King Arthur has left his mark on Cumbrian folklore as well as on the legends of Wales and Cornwall. One ballad claims that the king held court in 'Merry Carlisle', while some writers believe that the Roman bath-house at Ravenglass was the Arthurian Lyons Garde. Sadly, **King Arthur's Round Table** (qv) at Eamont Bridge is merely a prehistoric earthwork, but Armathwaite Castle is celebrated in ballad and romance as the site where Arthur slew the Giant of Castle Ewain beside Tarn Wathelayne. It has been suggested that Arthur's last battle of 'Camlen' was fought near Camboglanna, the fort on Hadrian's Wall, now called Birdoswald, and that Pendragon Castle, Mallerstang, is the legendary seat of Uther, Arthur's father. Uther Pendragon tried and failed to divert the River Eden to make a moat for his castle, which gives rise to the rhyme:

Let Uther Pendragon do what
    he can
Eden shall run as Eden ran

In 1835 Tennyson stayed with James Spedding at Mirehouse on the side of Bassenthwaite Lake, and it is thought that this visit inspired *Morte d'Arthur* and its tale of Excalibur — beloved of medievalists — drawn from the depths of the lake.

King Arthur's Round Table a late Neolithic-early Bronze Age earthwork near Eamont Bridge. It has no connection whatever with **King Arthur** (qv), though legend states that Sir Lancelot slew the mighty Tarquin somewhere in the vicinity. The monument is mentioned by Sir Walter Scott in his ***The Bridal of Triermain***.

king cough whooping cough (qv). The characteristic sound made by the sufferer from the complaint was known as ***kink***.

King's Evil Also known as scrofula, this skin complaint could be cured, it was believed, by a touch from the monarch. The first to 'touch for the Evil' was Edward the Confessor; the last was Queen Anne. Many Cumbrian parish account books contain references to parishioners being sent to London to be cured, and in 1669 Sir Daniel Fleming gave £10 to his brother Roger for the same purpose. The belief extended from the eleventh century to the eighteenth, and it has been argued that an element of psychosomatic medicine was involved. (see also *folk cures*)

King of Patterdale traditional hereditary title of the Mounsey family of Patterdale Hall. Legend said that the honour was originally acquired by members of the family who defeated a party of Border raiders at Stybarrow Crag on the shores of Ullswater.

kink (see *king cough*)

kinns chapped hands or cracks in the skin — usually cured by rubbing with warm tallow or, in the iron-mining areas, with tallow candles

kipper salmon out of season after spawning

kippertime between the 3rd and 12th May, during which salmon fishing was forbidden

kirk church (I *kirkja*, N *kirke*)

kirk-maister churchwarden

Kirkstone Pass Wordsworth wrote of a boulder 'whose church-like frame gives to this savage pass its name' — but which boulder? Opinions seem to differ.

Kirkstone Pass Inn licensed as a 'place of refreshment' in 1840 after the tragic deaths of some travellers crossing this high mountain pass in winter. It was built by that colourful Vicar of Troutbeck, **Parson Sewell** (qv), and an early

entry in the visitors' book reads:

The Sunday traveller on the
  Kirkstone Pass
Is bona fide and may have a glass.
So gentle stranger, do not stop
  to think,
Open your mouth, throw back your
  head and drink.
And while reposing 'neath the bleak
  fell-sides
As down your throat the nimble
  liquor glides,
Bless the kind parson who with
  these rude stones
Built this 'ere Inn to rest your
  weary bones

kissing bushes at Christmastime, two wooden hoops were formed into a rough sphere, and decorated with holly and ivy, and sugar apples (see *boolies*)

kist chest, such as a *bread kist*, a *linen kist* etc (I, ON *kista*, a chest)

kisty fastidious, squeamish (cf *picky*) (I *kveistinn*, fastidious, peevish)

kit small tub or bucket; milking pail

kite, kyte stomach; *gurt brossen* (qv) *kite!* is a term of abuse

kith ner kin (see *chick nor child*)

kittle to tickle, hence *kittlish*, ticklish; a *kittley cough* is a ticklish cough (I *kitla*, to tickle)

kittling kitten (I *kettlingur*, ON *kettling*, a kitten)

kizzened, kizzent dried up, withered, shrivelled *t' crabs* (qv) *is kizzened*

klockermungie (see *clockermunje*)

Knagg, Rev Richard This eighteenth century clergyman from

Eskew Head, near Tebay, is famous for his legendary — though incomplete — sermon given in the small and decrepit Dales church at Lunds. The pulpit was floored with sods from the churchyard, and when the good cleric began his address, he inadvertently disturbed an ants' nest — with predictable consequences. He is said to have left the pulpit hastily with the memorable words: '... the Devil has got into my breeches!'

knap hand cunning, skilful, handy *he's a knap hand wi' a gun*

kneap to tread down, for example, hay

knit-bone comfrey (see *bone setters*)

knitting sticks carved wooden knitting needle supports which were tucked into the belt around the waist. The needle was inserted into a hole in the end of the stick, holding it firm and so increasing the knitting speed. Traditionally these sticks were carved and given as a betrothal symbol, and often they show the date and initials. (see *Terrible Knitters of Dent*)

knocking-on getting older *Ah'm knocking-on tha knows*

knockin' trough stone trough used for bruising moist barley with a wooden pestle for making *frummety* (Wigton area)

knotty-tommies boiled milk to which oatmeal has been added to form lumps

knur and spell a game once popular in the late nineteenth century. A *knur* or round wooden

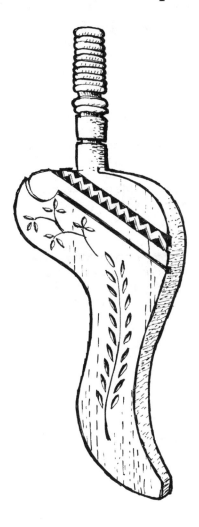

Knitting sticks were often carved as betrothal symbols.

ball was released from a *spell*, a spring trap; the *knur* was then immediately struck with a club known as a *pum stick* in an attempt to hit it as far as possible. The game was sometimes known as 'the poor man's golf'. (see also *piggy*)

kurn churn; A *stand kurn* was an 'up-an-down' churn

kyle (see *kile*)

kyne cattle (OE *cy*, cattle)

kyte (see *kite*)

A 'knur' ready for being sprung from the 'spell' and hit with the 'pum stick'. Knur and spell was a popular game in the late nineteenth century.

L

laal, lile little (N, D *lille*, little, small)

Laal Ratty affectionate name for the Ravenglass & Eskdale Railway

Laal Saffel Little Salkeld

laced tea tea to which rum has been added *sit thee down and we'll have oursels a dish o' laced tea*

Lady's Rake steep gulley on Walla Crag, Borrowdale, said to have been used by Lady Derwentwater during her supposed escape from Lord's Island after the failure of the 1715 Jacobite rebellion, in which her husband played a leading part and for which he was executed in 1716. The story goes on to relate that the good lady took her jewels and valuables with her. In the mid-nineteenth century a hoard of thirty-four silver pennies was discovered below the gulley, but they were all dated between 1272 and 1327, several centuries before her ladyship's athletic escapade (see *Lord Derwentwater's Lights*)

laen'd, leen'd sheltered place *yon's a leen'd spot for yows* (qv) *on t' fell* (High Furness) (see *lound*)

lafter, laghter brood of chickens; the eggs which a hen sits on during incubation (I *latr*, the place where animals lay their young)

laggy a childrens' term to indicate the last turn in a game (see also *bags, ferry*)

laid up incapacitated, confined to bed *Ah've bin laid up wi' a bad back* (cf *bed-fast*)

laik, laek to play games. According to De Quincey, Wordsworth used to make a pun on the double meaning of of this word — *laiking* meaning playing and *Laking* being the act of visiting the Lakes, a rare example of William's humour (I, ON *leika*, to play)

laikin child's toy (I *leikfang*, a toy)

lait, laet to search for, to seek (I *leita*, to seek, to search for)

laiting area from which people were *laited* or *bidden* (qv) to attend funerals, weddings, christenings etc (cf *bidding-round*)

Lake District National Park Established in 1951, the Lake District National Park is arguably the finest of Britain's National Parks. The 880 square miles (2,300 km²) make it the largest of the parks, and within its boundaries are England's highest

Lady's Rake on Walla Crag, Borrowdale.

mountain, Scafell Pike, and its deepest lake, Wastwater, as well as some of the finest fell and mountain scenery in Britain.

Lakeland Dialect Society was founded in 1939 to promote and encourage the speaking and understanding of Cumbrian dialect, and produces an annual journal

Lakers '... those persons who visit the beautiful scenes in Cumberland and Westmorland by distinction styled the Lakes' — *European Magazine*, 1798 (see also *laik*)

lam, lambast to beat soundly (I, ON *lemja*, to thrash, to beat)

Lampla Lamplugh

Lamplugh pudding toasted bread or biscuit steeped in warm ale, rum and spices (cf *powsowdy*)

lang long, hence Langdale and Langstrath (I *langur*, OE *lang*, long)

Langden Langdale

langlin' tying the forelegs of an animal together to prevent it from straying

lang sen, lang syne (north Cumbria) long since

And now you've a swatch (qv) *o'
    them good oald days
'At fwoak brags on as hevvin
    lang sen ...*

William Dickinson

langsom lonely, wearisome, oppressive, tiresome *it's a gay* (qv) *langsom road*

lang way much, considerably *it's a lang way better*

lant, lanter card game

lantern leets thin slivers of animal horn used as windows in a

Founded 1939

lantern, hence the expression *thin as lantern leets*

lap   to wrap up *Lap it in thi sark* (qv)

larn   to learn; also to teach *he larns his scholars to write* (see *dales larnin'*) (OE *leornian*, to learn, *laeran*, to teach)

larrup   to beat with a belt *he got a reet larrupin'*

last wolf in England   is said to have been killed near Humphrey Head, the limestone promontary jutting out into Morecambe Bay near Grange-over-Sands. Local tradition suggests that the hunter was Sir John Harrington of Wraysholme Tower, but sadly no date is specified.(see also **Wild Boar Fell**)

lat-axe   *riving* (qv) axe used by *swillers* (qv) (OE *latt*, a thin strip of wood)

lathe   barn, store (I *hlaða*, ON *hlatha*, a barn)

laverock   lark (ON *laevirke*, I *laevirki*, the lark)

lay   to arrange; *to lay the table* means to prepare the cutlery, etc (cf *set*)

laying out   act of preparing a body for burial, often undertaken by an elderly woman in the community (cf *streek*)

lead   to convey by cart, hence *leading hay* (OE *laedan*, to lead)

ledderin'   (see *tannin'*)

ledgers   highly localised childrens' game once played in certain terraced streets in the Hindpool area of Barrow. The aim was to hit with a ball a decorative line of bricks set in the wall at an angle of 45°; if successful, the ball would

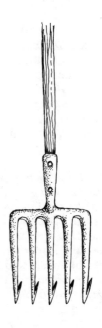

A salmon lester.

return to the server without bouncing. The server then moved back several paces and repeated the procedure. Kerb-side parking and increased traffic in the 1950s and 1960s meant the demise of the game — no doubt to the relief and delight of the residents.

leem   to remove kernels from the husks (see *brown leemers*)

leet on   to meet with by chance *he leet on 'im i' Kezzick* (qv)

leish, lash   to comb

lend   loan *gi' us a lend o' yer bat*

Lent   period from Ash Wednesday to Easter — preceded by *Collop Monday* (qv) — when certain traditions were respected (see *pace eggs*, *carlings*, *fig sue*)

lest unless *he'll be here soon, lest he's lost his way*

lester, leister, lister fish spear; for eels it has three flat serrated blades, for salmon, several barbed prongs (I *ljóster*, a salmon spear; N *lyster*, a fish spear)

let on to admit, to disclose, to reveal *Don't let on I told you, mind* (qv)

ley scythe; the term is used mainly in the central and south of the county (I *ljár*, N *lja*, a scythe)

lickin' physical punishment administered to a person or an animal

lift term associated with funerals; *what time do ye lift?* means what time will the cortège move off

lig to lie down, to lay (I *leggja*, to lay, place, put)

Ledgers — an urban street game.

99

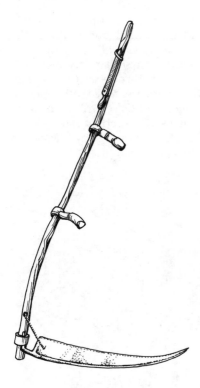

A ley and strickle.

liggan lying down

liggers long branches which a hedge-layer partly cuts through and then lays down to form a *dyke* (qv)

lile (see *laal*)

limmers pair of cart shafts (Low Furness) (cf *stang¹*) (ON *limar*, branches)

lines certificate of marriage, as in *weddin' lines*, a marriage certificate

lip impudence, cheek *Ah'll have none o' thi lip!*

lish active, nimble, sprightly *as lish as a trout*

lisk groin (ON *lysk*)

lister (see *lester*)

living over the brush living together without being married (see *besom*)

loand (see *lound*)

lobscouse type of stew formed of meat cut into small pieces and cooked with potatoes (N *lapskaus*, a stew)

lock number, quantity *a gay* (qv) *lock o' taties*

lonnin lane

loosenin' (see *lowzenin'*)

lop flea (ON *hloppa*, a flea)

lopper to curdle, to coagulate; milk turned sour is said to be *lopper't* (I *hlaup*, coagulated milk; ON *laupa*, to congeal)

Lord Derwentwater's Lights On the night of the execution of James Radcliffe, third and last Earl of Derwentwater, for his part in the first Jacobite Rebellion, the aurora borealis flashed with considerable intensity and clarity in the Keswick area, and therefore they were so named in remembrance of him. (cf *merry-dancers*, *streamers*) (see *Lady's Rake*)

louk to root up, to eradicate

loukin' tongs long-handled instrument for pulling up weeds and thistles in arable land. *Ah wouldn't tak hod on him wi' a par o' loukin tongs* — a variation on 'barge pole'.

lound, lown calm, sheltered, tranquil; in Cartmel, *loand* means quiet weather (cf *laen'd*) (I *logn*, calm)

loup, lowp to leap or jump. (ON *hlaupa*, OE *hleapan*, to leap)

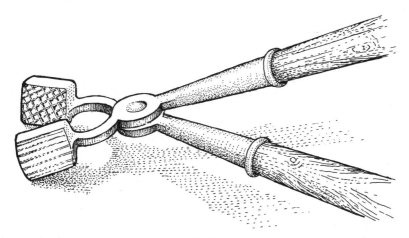

Loukin' tongs.

loupy-back game of leap-frog

loupy-dyke cow which is addicted to leaping over hedges (see *cow clog*) — but also used of a husband inclined to be unfaithful to his wife

low flame, blaze *keep thi fingers oot o' t' low!* (I *logi*, flame)

lowznin', lousin, loosenin' celebration held to mark the termination of an apprenticeship when the young man becomes a craftsman. It was customary for the friends of the former apprentice to invite local people to attend at the nearest inn; tea was served, and sports and dancing were held, and the profits were given to the young man to purchase the tools of his trade. (see also *time*)

luck penny small sum of money given back *fer luck* when a bargain is struck. In the nineteenth century this was generally a shilling a head on cattle. (cf *gift-again*)

lucks usually, but not exclusively, glass vessels which are regarded as safeguarding the luck or fortune of a house or a family. If broken or sold, the good fortune will depart. One of the best-known is the Luck of Edenhall, a thirteenth century enamelled glass vase, probably made in Aleppo and once owned by the Musgrave family. Associated with it was the rhyme:

If that glass should break or fall
Farewell the luck of Edenhall

Although the Luck remains intact in the Victoria and Albert Museum, the Musgraves died out and their hall was demolished in 1934. The Luck of Muncaster is a fifteenth century glass basin with white enamel mouldings, said to have been presented to Sir John Pennington by King Henry VI when he was given refuge at the castle after the Battle of Hexham.

Legend says that while the Luck remains unbroken, the Penningtons and their descendants will thrive. And perhaps the potency of the Luck is still present — the family were recently given a grant of money from English National Heritage to develop the castle and its grounds.

lucky bone small hammer-shaped sheep's bone once carried by children as a talisman (cf *cramp bone*)

lug¹ to drag or pull (N *lugge*, to pull by the hair)

lug² ear (see *lug marks*)

lug marks ownership marks on the ears of animals. The word is probably derived from the ON *lög*,

Established by Edward III in 1352, it lasted until the auction mart was created in the 1940s.

lum deep pool in a beck or stream where sheep were washed (cf *dub*)

lummakin heavy, awkward

lump it to put up with something *like it or lump it*

lying contests Temple Sowerby near Penrith was once famous for its lying contests, but by the nineteenth century the honours had gone to Wasdale Head where that old reprobate **Will Ritson** (qv), the landlord of the inn, won the title of the greatest liar in the world with his story of how he crossed his hounds with eagles to produce the fastest beasts in Lakeland —

FOLD BITTED	KEY BITTED	FORKED
RITTED	HALVED	PUNCHED
CROPPED	SNECK BITTED	SLIT
SHEAR HALVED	TWICE RITTED	STOVE FORKED

Some Cumbrian lug marks.

meaning law, ie a lawful mark, transposed to the place where the mark was made. *Lug marks* belong to the farm not the farmer. And generations of Cumbrian children have been threatened with *a clip round t' lug*. (see *smit books*)

Luke Fair held in Kirkby Stephen on St Luke's Day, the 27th October.

they had wings ...! The competition is still held in September; **Joss Naylor**, (qv) a former world champion, recently swept the board with a tale of crossing his *Herdwicks* (qv) with kangaroos, the resulting 'sheeparoos' being kept in the mother's pouch to protect them from foxes ...

M

maa[1] seagull (I *mávur*, a seagull)
maa[2] to mow, to cut down
maak, mawk maggot (I *maðkur*, ON *mathkr*, maggot, worm)
maak flee bluebottle
maekin yellow iris
maenjy, manegy, maungy peevish, pampered, surly

maezlin, mazlin someone with little sense, a *gaumless* (qv) individual
maddle, maffle to talk or act in a silly manner, to blunder, to mislead
Maffenby Maughenby
maiden clothes horse for drying clothes around an open fire

The maa.

main   (see *cock main*)

maint   may not

mak   kind, sort *oor mak o' toak*

mam   mother; *Give over or ah'll tell our mam* is a common Lancashire expression

mander, maunder   to talk in a confused manner

manishment   manure applied to fields

mannerly   decent, tidy, respectable *she's a gay mannerly body*

mapment, mopement   nonsense, silly talk, blundering

mappen, m'appen   perhaps
    'M'appen I may', she says,
        'm'appen I may;
    Thou thinks I believe the',
        an' m'appen I may!'
    Lal Dinah Grayson, A C Gibson
    (cf *happen*)

marbles   (see *taws[1]*)

Mardale   is one of the most evocative places in Cumbria, largely because of its history. **Alfred Wainwright** (qv) summed it up when he wrote: 'Mardale Green ... lost its life by drowning ... All that is left are ghosts'. Sacrificed to a thirsty Manchester, in 1936 the seventeenth century church was demolished and the remains of those who had rested beneath the shade of the ancient yew trees were reinterred at Shap. The same fate awaited the famous Dun Bull Inn, the home of the Mardale *shepherds' meet* (see also **Isaac Cookson**); the last gathering was held there in 1935 when, it is said, the *wake* (qv) continued from the Friday evening until the following Tuesday. In 1984 and again in 1995 the water level

of the Haweswater reservoir was so low that it was possible to stand within the churchyard and cross both Chapel Bridge and Arnold Bridge. For many this was an interesting and memorable experience; for the handful who had lived in the village, it was a sad and poignant occasion.

mardy   moody, sulky, spoilt (child); sometimes used to describe a dark, grey day *it's a mardy day*

markin' iron   branding iron for marking the horns of sheep and cattle

marra, marrer   companion, equal, a twin, literally 'the other one of a pair'; *marras* means 'two alike'. Generally associated with Northumbria but it is also found in West Cumbria and Furness, though here its use is declining. It was probably most closely associated with coal and iron mining communities.
    I needn't now say any meear,
    It's settled I'se ga'in to Barra, (qv)
    An' if I git back seaf an' sound,
    To this sang I'll send ye a marra
Poem printed in the *Ulverston Mirror*, September 1867.

marraless   not alike, not having a partner

marram grass   grows in sand dune locations around the coast. It was sometimes used in place of rushes for strewing on the church floors (see *rushbearing*). Kneeling on this sharp, spiky grass must have been a penance in itself!

Mary of Buttermere   Mary Robinson was the daughter of the innkeeper of the Fish, Buttermere,

Mary Robinson, the Maid of Buttermere.

at the end of the eighteenth century. She was seduced by John Hatfield, alias the 'Honourable Colonel Hope', who was neither a colonel or honourable — but he was certainly hopeful ... He was, in fact, a bigamist and a forger who was hanged outside Carlisle in 1803. Mary later married a Caldbeck farmer, Richard Harrison, and is buried in the churchyard there, just a stone's throw from the grave of **John Peel** (qv).

mash vat large vessel used for brewing ale

masher a toff (W Cumbria)

mass, mask, mash to infuse; *mash t' tea* is a request to brew the tea

mass dials Cumbria has not only the oldest known sundial in Britain (see **Bewcastle Cross**), it also has a number of so-called **mass dials** which operated on the same principle. It is believed that these vertical sundials marked the canonical hours, indicating when the church bell should be rung for services. Examples may be found at Caldbeck, Newbiggin, Torpenhow, Bolton-in-Westmorland, Urswick, Kirkoswald and some other places, but the finest examples are to be seen at the ancient church at Isel near Cockermouth. There are three on the jamb of the south window of the chancel — though one of these was originally intended as a horizontal dial and has been repositioned. Another, inside the porch, is located in a spot where the sun cannot reach, clearly indicating that the porch is a later addition.

maw see *maa¹*

May gezzlin, gozlin' similar to April Fool, but on the first day of May (see *gezzlins*)

May tree (see **hawthorn**)

mayor hunts ancient custom which combined a hunt with a *merry neet* (qv) The *mayor* was not a civic dignitary but a member of the community elected to lead the hunt and preside at the evening's entertainment. *Hunting mayors* held office in Ulverston in 1746, at Bowness (Windermere) in 1763, and at Troutbeck (Westmorland) where the first mayor, R Birkett, was elected in 1779. Today the Troutbeck hunt still survives, though this bastion of male chauvinism was breached in 1965-66 when Mrs C Clark was elected mayor. In 1986-87 the fourth lady mayor, Rachel Freeman, was appointed.

mayzel, maze to stupify, to confuse

mazelins, mayzlins silly, stupid creatures

meeaster, maister master, boss; sometimes used in the sense of 'husband', eg *'I fund him at t' Black Bull, wi' yower meeaster an' a lock* (qv) *meear o' t' seeam sooart', Betty Yewdale* (qv) by A C Gibson

meerstan, meerstone boundary stone, stone landmark

meetings meeting of two tidal currents, producing rough and dangerous conditions for small craft — eg Walney Meetings

mek make *Mek lively!* means 'Shape up!' or 'Hurry up!'

melder quantity of grain ground at one time; quantity of meal or flour (I *meldur*, meal)

melgreaves quicksands (Cartmel) (ON *melr*, a place full of sand)

mell[1] wooden mallet; also the prize given for the last in any competition, the modern expression being 'the wooden spoon' (OF *mail*)

mell[2] final cut of corn in the harvest field. Traditionally this was plaited, enclosing a large

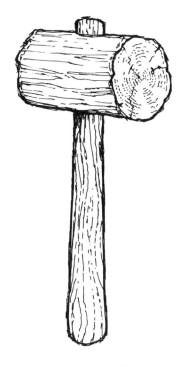

A wooden mell.

apple, and hung in the farmhouse until Christmas morning, when the corn was given to the best cow and the apple to the oldest farm servant. (cf *Kersmas sheaf*)

mell passage short passage, about six feet (2m) long, which led from the *hallan* (qv) to the *fire house* (qv) (cf *heck*[2])

mell supper (see *kern supper*)

Mellerby Melmerby

mend to improve in health *Ah've bin badly* (qv) *but noo ah'm on t' mend.* Also used in the sense of to improve or tend: *mend t' fire* means to add more fuel to the fire

mense manliness, tact, propriety, decency, neatness, order

menseless unseemly, lacking in dignity; the opposite of *mense* (qv)

merrils (see *Nine Men's Morris*)

merry-begatan, merry-begot illegitimate child (cf *chance barn*)

merry-dancers Northern Lights, or aurora borealis (cf *Lord Derwentwater's Lights, merry-dancers, streemers*)

merry neet social gathering held on such occasions as Christenings, Christmas, the completion of a *clay daubin* (qv), a *timber raising* (qv) or a *boon ploughing* (qv). Usually it involved feasting, drinking, dancing, singing and card-playing. Sadly — and unaccountably — the term *merry neet*, once synonymous with Cumbrian folk culture, has been replaced by the gaelic word *ceilidh*.

Messenger, Mally (1763–1856) born in Watendlath and ran a dame's school in Keswick. Described as an 'ancient sybil, bending her thin face and brown antique features and unspectacled eyes on the Sacred Book', she had nevertheless been *lish* (qv) and athletic in her youth. She had competed in — and won — foot races organised by **Joseph Pocklington** (qv) as part of his Keswick **Regattas** (qv), and on several occasions she walked to London and back. On one such visit she bought a small table and carried it back to Keswick on her shoulders ...

metal   quarryman's term for slate[1] (qv)

mew, moo   stack of loose hay

mickle   large, great; as in Mickledore, the gap between Scafell and Scafell Pike, and Mickleden at the head of Great Langdale (I *mikill*, ON *mikkel*, large)

> *Many littles make a mickle*
> *Many mickles make a mile*
> old rhyme

usually associated with health, as in *Nay, ah'm nobbut* (qv) *middlin'*. When **John Dalton** (qv), the Cumbrian-born scientist, was presented at Court, King William IV asked the good doctor how things were in Manchester; *'Very middlin', I think'*, came the reply.

miff-maff   nonsense

Miller, John Fletcher   Born in Whitehaven, throughout his life Miller (1816-1856) kept a detailed record of local weather. Using thirty-five rain guages throughout the Lake District, he was able to determine that Sty Head had the unenviable reputation as the wettest place in England. He was made a Fellow of the Royal Society in 1850.

miller thumb   willow wren

mim   prim, precise

mind[1]   to remember, to take care (to do something), largely used in

Many a little makes a Mickle.

AT a Time like the present when every Article requisite in Housekeeping is so dear that Labourers and Mechanics, who have large Families to support, can scarcely make both Ends meet,

middert, middlemer   middle in relation to size, age, position etc.

middlin'   average. The word is

the north and the west of the county *Mind ta think on* (qv), *now!* (I *minna*, to remind)

mind² an exclamation *Mind this-sen*(qv)*!* means 'Get out of the way!

mirk dark, dusk (I *myrkur*, darkness, gloom)

missel, missen myself

mitey cheese infested with maggots

mizzle¹ fine rain

mizzle² to swindle, mislead, slink away

moider, moither, mither to stupify, bewilder, embarrass, confuse, pester

mollycoddle to spoil with excessive care and attention *Nay, tha's mollycoddlin' t' lad!*

montikitty, mounty-kitty game in which one boy leant against a high wall, another would climb onto his shoulders and a third boy would leap onto them both — and so on, until the whole thing collapsed. Regional variations of the same game are *bull loup*, *high cockalorum*, *kicking donkey*, *pund o' mair weight* and *stick-a-roger* (qv).

moo (see *mew*)

moonleet flit (see *flit*)

mooter meal or flour claimed by the miller as his fee for grinding the grain

Moreville, Sir Hugh de (?–1202) One of the more infamous of the twelfth century Cumbrian knights. As well as building Pendragon Castle and strengthening Brough Castle, he was one of the assassins of Thomas à Becket in 1170. Tradition says that he held back the crowd with his sword while Becket was murdered in Canterbury Cathedral. Hugh's Seat, near

to the source of the River Eden, is thought to have been named after him.

Morlan floods flooding in the Keswick area which often coincided with the Feast of St Mary Magdalen (22nd July), hence the name and the rhyme:
Morlan flood
Ne'er did good

Morocco name given to an exceptionally potent beer once brewed at Levens Hall, south of Kendal. The recipe was said to have been introduced by one Howard, a Crusader, and it was supposed to be kept for twenty-one years before tapping. The ingredients are secret, but one description records that it was 'almost dark, pours like oil, and tastes mild as milk in its treachery'. Pure Genius?

morris men (see *pace egg song*)

mortal an indefinitive term often used to add force to an expression *a mortal long way*

Mortal Man Inn This inn in Troutbeck is one of the best known of the Lakeland hostelries. It was built in 1689 and is famous for its sign which states:
O Mortal Man, that lives by bread,
What is it makes thy nose so red?
Thou silly fool that looks so pale,
'Tis drinking Sally Birkett's ale

morts¹ young salmon on their first return from the sea

morts² girls (Wigton area). Probably a Romany term.

mossberries cranberries (cf *crones*)

mossing the church regarded as a boon (free) service, *mossing the church* involved the filling of the cracks in the roof with moss to keep out the weather

motty peg central stake around which the *shanklings* (qv) were stacked in a charcoal *pitstead* (qv)

moudewarp, moudywarp mole (I *moldvarpa*, N *moldvarp*, the mole)

A moudewarp.

mounty-kitty (see *montikitty*)

muck hack, muck-drag three-pronged rake for drawing manure from a cart (cf *gripe*)

muck hots panniers for carrying manure on horseback (see *holts*)

muffatee knitted woollen cuffs for the wrists

mugg cross between a Leicester and a Fell sheep

muggy close and drizzly weather

mull to crumble into dust, also small particles and fragments such as *peat mull*

mum silent; to *keep mum* is to remain silent

mummers group of actors, mostly in disguise (see *pace egg song*)

mun[1] mouth *Shut thi mun!* (cf, *gab*, *gob*) (I *munnur*, mouth)

mun[2] must

mun't, moan't, mau't must not *Thoo mau't gang awae till thoo's shutten this yatt!*

              sign on a gate in Crosby Ravensworth

murrain foot-and-mouth disease (see *needfire*)

murrey dark red dye used in the Kendal cloth industry, made by boiling lichen

Musgrave, Sir Thomas (1737–1812) was born at Hayton overlooking the Solway Firth. He fought with distinction in the American War of Independence and was the last British Commandant of New York. He is buried at St George's Church, Hanover Square in London.

musical stones stone xylophones made from a type of local slate (see *whintin*). Peter Crosthwaite (qv), the eighteenth century Keswick Museum curator, is thought to be one of the first to exhibit this type of instrument. They became quite popular in the nineteenth century, and a stone xylophone band had the honour of playing before Queen Victoria — literally the first rock group!

Myers, William according to his memorial stone in the Piper Choir of Cartmel Priory, died on the unlikely date of the 30th February 1762.

N

naff, nave hub of a cartwheel (see also *fellies*) (OE *nafa*, hub of a wheel)

nag rake drag rakes used in the making of hay (cf *old mare, donkey rake*)

naggel to gnaw (I *naga*, to gnaw)

narhand near to

narmest nearest

narst, narsta nearly *Ah was narsta kilt*

natter long chat, gossip

nay no — but more definite than a simple negative

Naylor, Joss Wasdale farmer and former World Champion Liar (see **lying contests**), but most famous as one of the finest **fell runners** (qv) in Britain. One of his greatest achievements was running to the summits of seventy-two Lakeland peaks, each over 2,000 feet (610m) high, in 23 hours and 11 minutes — an amazing feat of endurance. And to celebrate his sixtieth birthday in 1996 he undertook a charity run and bagged sixty peaks in 36 hours and 57 minutes. He was awarded an MBE for his services to this most masochistic sport.

neaf, neef, neave fist (ON *nefi*, I *hnefi*, OE *neve*, a fist)

near mean, stingy, parsimonious, tight-fisted *Ah's nut gaan to that shop — they're varra near*

neavy-nack childrens' game of casting lots; guessing which hand contains the object

Neavy, neavy nack
Which hand will ye tak?

(see *neaf*)

neb bill, beak or nose; peak of a cap; cape or promontory *keep tha neb out o' it!* (OE *nebb*, nose, beak)

needfire primitive form of fumigation which was believed would cure *murrain* or foot-and-mouth disease in cattle. All fires in a community were extinguished and fire was kindled by friction in some central spot; smoke was encouraged by heaping on green leaves, after which the cattle were driven through the *reek* (qv). Harriet Martineau tells of one farmer who, after treating his beasts, sent his ailing wife through the smoke! The last recorded use of *needfire* was at Troutbeck in 1851. (probably derived from *neat*, an ox, cow or bull)

Needfire, a primitive attempt to cure 'murrain'.

neet hawk nightjar

ner nor, than *yon's bigger ner tuther* (qv) (cf *nor*)

nesh delicate (OE *nesce*)

nesp to nip off the stalks and withered flowers from gooseberries

nibs small handles attached to the shaft of a *ley* (qv)

Nicholson, Norman Cumbria's other great poet. For almost all his life Norman Nicholson (1914–1987) lived in St George's Terrace, Millom. Rejoicing in the description 'a local poet', he lovingly chronicled the landscape, geology, natural history and people of his native county. He was awarded the Queen's Medal for Poetry in 1977.

Nicolson, Bishop William (1655–1727) noted antiquarian and Bishop of Carlisle. In 1715, during the first Jacobite invasion, he and Lord Lonsdale attempted to rally the untrained Cumbria militia on Penrith Fell. Being mostly armed with billhooks and pitchforks, the rabble were no match for the Highlanders and they soon took to their heels; Lord Lonsdale galloped off to Lowther, leaving the good bishop in his coach-and-six. His coach driver, believing that discretion was the bettter part of valour, whipped up the horses and carried his reverend and gallant master back home to Rose Castle. The bishop, it is said, lost his episcopal wig when shouting out of the carriage window, prompting the rhyme by Thomas Sanderson:

The Bishop gain'd his snug retreat,
Thank'd Heaven he breathed the air;
And all his bliss had been complete,
Had not his head been bare

For ah! when on a length of road
His troubles waxed great,
The thatch, which hat and wig bestow'd
Unkindly left his pate!

niggert iron cheeks placed in the fire grate to reduce its width and so save fuel

nigh on nearly *Ah'm nigh on eighty tha' knows*

night owl one who stays up late at night

Nine Men's Morris popular early medieval board game, possibly first introduced by the Irish-Norse peoples or the Normans. It is also called *merrils*, from the Old French word *marelle,* meaning a token or counter. There is a fine example inscribed into the first step at the entrance of the ruined guesthouse in Furness Abbey, but whether or not this pre- or post-dates the dissolution is unknown.

Nine Standards nine drystone cairns on the fell above the village of Hartley. The tradition in the Eden Valley suggests that they were put there to deceive an enemy into thinking that they were the vanguard of an advancing army, but the truth is less romantic — they simply marked the boundary between Westmorland and Yorkshire.

nip minute quantity; also a pinch with the fingers — *nip fer new*

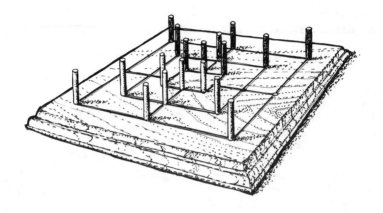

Nine Men's Morris, or 'merrils', was a popular early medieval board game.

was a pinch administered when a person wore new clothes for the first time

nip up to pilfer, to pick up quickly, to get a bargain

nobbut only *'Who's that?' 'It's nobbut me — let's in'*. One of John Richardson's (qv) best-known poems is called *It's nobbut me*, and a poem by Norman Nicholson (qv) bears the title *Nobbut God*. (OE *nan-beutan*, only)

noggin small liquid measure, approximately a quarter of a pint (150ml) . The Hawkshead Parish Accounts for 1689 relate the story of three apprentices who went out for a 'night on the tiles'. William Braithwaite and William Stamper made a bet with Bernard Swainson that he could not drink 'nine noggins of brandy'. If he did, the other two would pay, but if he failed he would have to pay for whatever he managed to consume. Bernard did manage to drink the nine noggins:

'... and shortly after that fell downe upon the floore; and was straightway carried to his bed where hee layed two and twenty hours; dureinge which time hee could never speke, noe, nor never did know any body though many Came to See him and Soe he dyed.'

nor than *it's bigger nor tudder* (qv) (see *ner*)

norry boat the seven stars making up the constellation of the Plough or Great Bear. Perhaps a reference to Noah's ark? (Cartmel)

nought at dow good for nothing

nowt nothing *If thoo knows nowt, say nowt; if thoo knows summat, say less* — old Cumbrian saying

nowther — ner neither — nor; *it's nowther nowt* (qv) *ner summat* means it is neither one thing or the other

O

oatbread (see *clapbread, haver bread*)

obbut except, all but *he fund 'em — obbut yan* (qv)

off going *Ah'm off yam* (qv)

offcums, offcomers strangers, people who are not natives

olas always

Old Christmas Day The change in the calendar in 1752 and the 'loss' of eleven days meant that the 5th January became 'Old' Christmas Day. In Cumbria it was believed that at midnight on 'Old' Christmas Eve, the bees in their hives began to buzz in celebration of the birth of the Christ Child and the cattle knelt in their stalls.

old mare, 'od meare large wooden rake used to gather ears of corn after harvest (cf *nag rake*)

old men's workings used in Cumbrian mines and quarries to describe the workings of former miners and quarrymen

o-maks all kinds, all makes

omert densely shaded by trees

on of *they're marras* (qv) — *two on a kind*

on t' rwoad on the way, ie pregnant *she's on t' rwoad*

oo' (see *woo'*)

Oofer Ulpha

Oostan, U'stan Ulverston

orchan (see *urchin*)

Ossalinsky, Countess spirited member of the Jackson family of Armboth Hall, Thirlmere, who married a Russian count. On becoming a widow, the countess returned home and carried out a rearguard action against Manchester Corporation Waterworks Committee when they proposed creating their reservoir in the late nineteenth century. Manchester valued the Countess's estate at £25,000; she, however, had a more inflated figure in mind and in 1882, after legal action, she was awarded £70,000, though it is believed that she finally accepted a figure somewhat less than the award.

Otley, Jonathan (1766–1856) watch and clock repairer, engraver, guidebook writer, meteorologist, botanist and geologist. Born near Loughrigg Tarn, Jonathan Otley moved to Keswick in 1791, became a friend of **John Dalton** (qv), the chemist and originator of the atomic theory, and the great geologist, Adam Sedgwick. Acknowledged as the father of Lake District geology, Otley not only recognised the three major division of Lakeland rocks — the Skiddaw Slates, the Borrowdale Volcanic rocks and the Silurian Slates — he was also the first person to scientifically investigate the **Floating Island of Derwentwater** (qv). (see *dales larnin'*)

out-foxed out-witted. In March 1994, twenty-four hounds belonging to the Ullswater Hunt became *crag-fast* (qv) overnight on a *bink* (qv) on St Sunday Crag — and had to be rescued by the Patterdale Mountain Rescue team. A true case of being *out-foxed* and no doubt the fox had the last laugh! (see **foxhunting**)

out o' fettle not well, not useable (see *fettle*)

out o' sorts sulky, peevish, 'off-colour'

outrake narrow passage from enclosed land to the common (OE *rayke*, to wander about)

overins removable top rim around the sides of a cart, used to increase the capacity (cf *shelvins*)

over-blown sheep buried in a snowdrift

ower-by near to *he lives ower by Seathet*

ower-faced to give too much to eat *nay, ah'm ower-faced* (cf *full up¹*)

ower-kessen'd overcast, cloudy, gloomy

owl hole small hole in the eaves of the gable end of a barn to allow

Oxeye.

the exit and entrance of owls. *Hullets* (qv) were to be encouraged because they helped to keep down vermin. (see *jenny hole*)

own'd recognised *Nay, tha's grown! Ah wadn't own'd ye if ye hedn't spokken*

owt anything *we're fair clemmed* (qv) — *we'll eat owt!* (OE *awiht*, anything)

owt like reasonable, fit (often referring to weather) *if it's owt like, we'll away to Gersma* (qv) *Sports*

oxeye marguerite daisy

oxter armpit, except in Furness and Cartmel where *armhole* was used (OE *oxta*, armpit)

P

pace eggs hard-boiled eggs coloured with redwood dye, alum or onion skins. Skilled practitioners would write their names on the shells in molten candle wax before dyeing, and this would then appear white on the finished eggs. The eggs would then be displayed in house windows until Easter, when traditionally children would gather at some appropriate spot — the castle moat at Penrith, Castle Hill in Kendal, Hoad Hill in Ulverston — and the eggs would be bowled against one another like some giant conker game. When the Wordsworths lived at Rydal Mount, their *pace eggs* were decorated for them by Robert Dixon, the gardener, and his efforts may be seen in the Dove Cottage Museum in Grasmere. (*pace* is a corruption of *paschal*, meaning Easter)

pace egg song song and dance still performed by *morris men*, *Jolly Boys* or *mummers* in various parts of Cumbria. The characters include Lord Nelson, Tosspot, the Doctor and Bessy Brownbags, and the opening doggerel runs:

Here's two or three Jolly Boys all
*   in one mind,*
We've come a pace egging, and
*   hope you'll prove kind,*
We hope you'll prove kind with
*   your eggs and strong beer,*
And we'll come no more nigh you
*   until the next year*

Pace eggs, hard-boiled and either dyed or painted, are still part of Easter festivities in Cumbria.

packhorses Within the steeply-sloping central Cumbrian fells, packhorses proved to be the most sensible and efficient method of transport, and by 1770 a network of packhorse trains linked Whitehaven, Cockermouth, Penrith, Ulverston, Hawkshead and Cartmel with Kendal, which rapidly became the most important packhorse centre between Wigan and Scotland. It is estimated that about 230 packhorses were regularly entering and leaving this grey

Monk's Bridge, a packhorse bridge near Calder Abbey.

Westmorland market town each week — a clear measure of its importance. The last packhorse route, linking Kendal with Whitehaven over Wrynose and Hardknott passes, was still in use in the late nineteenth century. (see packhorse bridges)

packhorse bridges are narrow, single-arch structures which originally lacked walls, since these would catch on the loaded panniers. Many have subsequently been widened and the evidence may be seen by looking underneath the bridge — eg **Doctor's Bridge** (qv) in Eskdale. Some, such as Monk's Bridge over the River Calder, may be medieval, but the majority seem to have been built between 1660 and 1760. Only one, Calva Hall Bridge over the River Marron, has a dated stone, 1697.

packin' *to send packin'* is to dismiss someone summarily

packmen (see **Scotchmen**)

paddle to trample underfoot

paddock toad (I *padda*, N *padde*, a toad)

paddock steal toadstool; all non-edible fungi

paggered exhausted *Me legs was paggered* (cf *jiggered*)

paik severe beating, usually given by a schoolmaster

pain-lookers officers of the manorial court who were responsible for the pains and penalties imposed. On Walney Island *pain lookers* were appointed to see that the sluices in the sea defence dikes were in good repair, while at Troutbeck, the *Painable Fence Book*, first written in 1680, records the length of boundary wall between Ambleside and Troutbeck which had to be maintained by each tenant.

pant cesspit

Pardza Pardshaw

parin' spade (see *push plough*)

parlish remarkable, wonderful, extraordinary

pash fall, a downfall a *girt pash o' rain*

passing bell audible signal on the church bell to indicate to the community who was about to be buried. In Troutbeck the bell tolled nine times for a man, six for a woman and three for a child.

paste eggs (see *pace eggs*)

Pavey Ark in Great Langdale is thought to have been the scene of one of the most remarkable mountain 'rescues' ever recorded. The Ark is a precipitous rock face towering above Stickle Tarn. On the 7th November 1797 that irrepressible tourist, Captain Joseph Budworth, determined to climb the Langdale Pikes, accompanied by a local fifteen year old shepherd boy, Paul Postlethwaite. The pair experienced no difficulty in ascending the mountain — but on the descent Budworth became seriously frightened for, in his own words, young Paul had led him across 'a sward nearly perpendicular, and of immoderate height'. At this point Captain Budworth, who had only one arm (he had lost the other at the siege of Gibraltar some years earlier), almost became *crag-fast*(qv), but he overcame his attack of vertigo by taking out his handkerchief and tying it over his right eye to prevent him seeing the drop on that side. With his good arm, he held out his walking stick to Paul Postlethwaite who, no doubt gingerly, led him to safety. It has been argued that the site of this escapade was Jack's Rake, the diagonal *trod* (qv) which crosses the face of Pavey Ark.

pearl gathering This apparently unlikely activity was once locally important at the mouth of the River Irt, where seed pearls could — and still can — be found in mussels. Camden mentions that the shellfish were gathered at low water and the resulting 'shell-berries' were bought by jewellers from 'the poor people for a trifle but [they] sell them at a good profit'. In 1695 a company was formed to search for pearls in the Irt, and Mr Thomas Patrickson of How Hall, Ennerdale, employed people to gather these seed pearls, which he sold in London for the princely sum of £800.

peat barrow wheelbarrow with a broad wheel to prevent it from sinking in the soft peat

peat pot a peat working. A *pot* usually produced two types of peat; the upper fibrous layers were *grey peats*, used for kindling; the lower *black peats* were more valuable and gave more heat when burned. (see also *grave*, *toppins*, *turbary*)

peat spade usually made of wood, with a metal cutting edge

which had a flange at right angles to the toe of the spade, allowing a vertical and a horizontal cut with one movement (cf *slane*)

peatus, peat scale stone-built hut for the storage of peat

peedle to look slyly about

peeky sick, ill *he's looking a lile bit peeky*

Peel, John The most famous of all huntsmen, John Peel (1777–1854) was born at Park End, near Caldbeck. His coat was *hodden grey* (qv), and by all accounts he was *'terrible lang (qv) in t' leg and lish (qv) with a fine girt neb (qv) and grey eyes that could see for ivver'*. His devotion to hunting was such that on the same day his son, Peter, died, he joined the hunt and brought back a 'brush' which was duly buried in the coffin. Peel himself was 'run to earth' at Ruthwaite in 1854. (see *D' ye ken John Peel?*)

Peerith Penrith

A peat barrow.

John Peel, the most famous Cumbrian huntsman, in his coat of 'hodden grey'.

A peat spade or 'slane'.

peg rugs made from various pieces of coloured woollen rags prodded through a piece of hessian with a wooden peg. Elaborate designs and pictures were frequently made. They were also known as *rag rugs* and *proddy rugs*.

pelt, pell heavy shower of rain or hail. A Cumbrian, on being asked if it rained much in his neighbourhood, replied *'It donks and drizzles, but nivver cums doon in nea girt pell'*.

penny ale fair eighteenth and early nineteenth century gathering at ale houses, where men and women each paid a penny into a kitty which was then used to buy ale

phizzick medicine or tonic of any kind

picking on to victimise *teacher's allus pickin' on me*

pickle a condition of difficulty or confusion *aye, it's a reet pickle*

picky over-particular, or hard to please *Bairn's picky wi' its scran* (qv) (cf *kisty*)

piece slice of bread, butter and jam *mam* (qv), *can I 'ave a piece and play out?* (used in Barrow and district; probably an imported word from central and south Lancashire)

pigeon feathers In the eighteenth and early nineteenth centuries, there was a curious belief that a dying person could not pass away peacefully if he or she was lying on a bed containing pigeon feathers. When death appeared to be imminent, the patient was often removed from the bed and placed on the floor; such uncouth handling frequently hastened the arrival of the Grim Reaper — thereby adding credibility to the superstition!

pigeon flyers sycamore seeds (cf *jinny spinners*)

piggin stave-built vessel, about the size of a breakfast cup. One of the staves was longer than the rest and this served as a handle.

piggy game in which a stick, pointed at both ends, is struck, causing it to fly into the air. It is then hit as far as possible. A variation of **knur and spell** (qv).

pike (see *stye*)

pikethank hanger-on (Cartmel)

pilgarlic foolish person, simpleton

pill-gill *quack doctor's* (qv) display; any show at a fair or market; a term of contempt

pilliver pillow

pinnel boulder clay left by the glaciers (south Cumbria)

pinner't shrivelled, lean, starved

pintallin' (see *fisslen about*)

pippins pips of apples or pears. Traditionally used to determine in which direction a future wife or husband lay. The pip was squeezed between the finger and the thumb until it flew, and the following rhyme was repeated:

A piggin.

Pippin, pippin paradise
Tell me where my love lies;
East, west, north, south
Kirkby, Kendal, Cockermouth?

pissibed dandelion. The name is derived from the well-known attribute of this plant. The white sap, if applied to warts, was believed to remove them. (cf *dogstinks*)

pissimires ants (OE *pisse-myre* from the urine smell of an anthill, but also I, N *maur*, S *myra*, an ant)

pitsteads circular charcoal-burning floors between 10-20 feet (3-6m) across. On sloping ground, the **pitsteads** were often cut into the hillside and banked up with spoil on the opposite side to create a level floor. Sometimes known as **pit-rings**. (see also **motty peg**, **say**, **shanklings**)

play-jigg play written in rhyme (see **Hoggart, Thomas**)

ploat to pluck feathers from the carcass a bird (eastern Cumbria) (cf **pull**)

plug-and-feather quarryman's tools for *riving* (qv) slate[1] (qv) (see also *dressing brake*, **whittle**)

plumbago (see **wad**)

poap to walk aimlessly

pobs, pobbies bread and milk; food for infants

Pocklington, Joseph Although an *offcomer* (qv), Joseph Pocklington became one of the great eighteenth century Cumbrian eccentrics. A man of 'private means', 'King Pocky' bought Derwent Island in Derwentwater in 1778, and immediately began the construction of a large house and several attendant follies such as a boathouse in the style of a Non-conformist chapel, a mock church, a paste-board battery complete with cannon, and a 'Druid's Temple' of standing stones. With **Peter Crosthwaite** (qv), he was the instigator and organiser of the Derwentwater Regatta. (see **Bowder Stone, regattas**)

poddish form of oatmeal porridge, believed to be a health-giving food

You ask me why so lish (qv) *I go 'T was poddish, barn* (qv)*, that made me so!*

H D Rawnsley

(cf *hasty pudding*)

poddish kite gluttonous child or youth

poke[1] cone-shaped bag, often made from a twist of paper, used to contain sweets; a pouch or small sack. Dorothy Wordsworth uses the term in her *Journal*. (I *poki*, a bag)

poke[2]**, pouk** boil or pimple

poor man's golf (see *knur and spell*)

posser implement used to agitate clothes in a boiler. It consists of a long wooden handle with a concave copper head pierced with holes. (see *dolly legs*)

posset boiled milk to which ale has been added

pots any kind of crockery *side* (qv) *t' pots from t' table*

pot oven (see *kale pot*)

pot skar fragment of broken pottery (N *potteskar*, pot-sherd)

potter to dawdle, to saunter at a job

Potter, Beatrix A Londoner by birth, Beatrix Potter (1866–1943) had an early tenuous link with Cumbria — her paternal grandfather had been a Liberal MP for Carlisle. Best known for her childrens' stories of anthropomorphic animals, she was also an excellent botanical illustrator and, later, a breeder and judge of **Herdwick** sheep (qv). Renouncing her blue-stocking Kensington background, she adopted Cumbrian dress, and was often seen at sheep fairs in a battered felt hat and with a sack around her shoulders. On one occasion she encountered a tramp near Windermere ferry who announced *'Aye, missus — times is bad fer t' likes o' thee and me'*. It is said that local children were

A posser — a useful washday implement.

somewhat afraid of her and, like Mr McGregor in *The Tale of Peter Rabbit*, she would think nothing of chasing boys who stole her apples! Her generosity to the National Trust was legendary, and by her death she had given more than 4,000 acres (1,600ha) and a number of farms to the trust.

Beatrix Potter.

potty common clay marble (see *taws¹*)

pour (see *teem*)

powcat¹ polecat or foumart

powcat² stinkhorn fungus

powsowdy Brewed for Christmas and other festive occasions, *powsowdy* was ale boiled with rum and bread, seasoned with spices, nutmeg and sugar. The bread, eaten as a kind of dessert, was

known in west Cumberland as *Lamplugh pudding* (qv). (cf *humming grog*)

prease to invite (Cartmel); *you'll need no preasin'* means 'you will need no invitation'

proddle to poke, to make holes in something

proddy rugs (see *peg rugs*)

public wedding (see *bidden wedding*)

puddin-kite unfledged bird

puddin' poke linen bag in which *Easterledge pudding* (qv) was boiled

puddled muddy *t' field's allus puddled at t' back end* (qv)

pull to pluck feathers from a bird, except in Furness and Cartmel where the term *pluck* is used, and in the east of the county where *ploat* (qv) is more common

pum stick striking stick used in *knur and spell* (qv)

pund o' mair weight (see *montikitty*)

punt small, heavy, clinker-built, boat rowed with two ash oars or a single oar at the stern (see *sculling*). Far removed from the flat-bottomed boats traditionally used by undergraduates on the River Cam. (Low Furness)

purlock dirty wool

purly post spinning top used in games. It was marked on its four sides:

T   *tak yan away*
P   *put yan down*
S   *sweep o' away*
L   *let it alean*

push plough crude, man-operated plough similar to a pointed

A push plough — 'the most slavish work in husbandry'.

A pyat or pyannet.

spade with a flange at right angles to the face, which acted as a coulter. The shaft was usually six feet (2m) long, terminated by a cross-piece 'crown' which was pushed by the operator's chest or thighs. It was used on steep slopes to pare off turf, which was then burned and the ashes forked into the ground. On difficult terrain, a second man might be harnessed to the 'plough' like a draught animal. Not surprisingly, such work has been described as 'the most slavish work in husbandry'.

(cf *parin' spade*) (see also *rowan-tree plough*)

put on[1] to sustain someone until a full meal can be provided *this'll put me on till ah gits yam* (qv)

put on[2] oppressed, taken advantage of, hen-pecked (of a man) *Sitha!* (qv) *Don't let her put on thee!*

put out ashamed, troubled *he was put out by t' sneck posset* (qv)

put wood in t' 'ole kindly close the door

pyat, pyannet magpie

Q

quack doctors All Cumbrian **hiring fairs** (qv) and markets were visited by mountebanks or *quack doctors*. Amongst the most popular remedies were Kendal Black Drop (almost certainly containing laudanum), toothache drops, baby tantrum powder, Balm of Gilead, the Reverend John Wesley pills, a nostrum called Green Fire to ward off colds and chills, and an infusion named Virgin Water, 'guaranteed to preserve that state in the imbiber'. (see *pill-gill*, *toothpullers*)

Quakerism had its first missionary centre at Swarthmoor, near Ulverston. George Fox, the founder of the movement, first came here in 1652, and although his fiery preaching aroused hostility in some areas — he survived an assassination attempt on Walney Island — others were converted by the force of his personality. Under the patronage of Judge Fell, the owner of Swarthmoor Hall, Fox increased his conversions; Margaret Fell and her daughters soon joined the Friends, but the judge remained a member of the Church of England until his death in 1658. From the hall the first organised missionary tours were planned and carried out, and the so-called 'Valiant Sixty' began their journeys from here. Like so many Friends, Margaret Fell suffered imprisonment in Lancaster Castle for her beliefs. After eleven years of widowhood, she married George

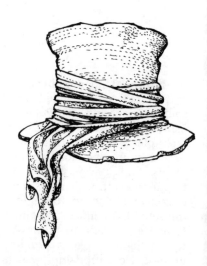

The origin of the phrase 'As queer as Dick's hatband' is obscure.

Fox in 1669. He died in 1691 and is buried in London; she survived at Swarthmoor until 1702 and is buried in an unmarked grave at Sunbrick, overlooking Morecambe Bay.

queer as Dick's hatband odd, strange, morose, sullen. The phrase is also common in Yorkshire and Lancashire, though its origin is obscure.

queer do something which is strange or unusual *it was a reet queer do* (cf *rum do*)

quindam a fifteenth. In Furness and Cartmel, which were both in Lancashire until 1974, county taxes were based on *quindams*. Even as late as 1826 the Walney Island poor rate was assessed as '400 quindams'.

quit free; in a game of chance, *double or quits* means double the debt or free from any obligation (I *kvittr*, free)

quittance receipt *Ah'll not pay without a quittance* (I *kvittun*, a receipt)

R

rabbit smoot small hole left in the base of a **drystone wall** (qv) through which rabbits had access to fields. On one side of the wall, a slate-lined pit covered over with a hinged board was strategically placed; when the retaining pin was removed from the board, the rabbits then fell into the trap — and rabbit pie was on the menu the following day! (N *smau*, a narrow passage)

rabblement rabble

rackencrook (see *rattencrook*)

rackle hasty, rash, incautious

rackups consequences of misconduct or defeat *he mun* (qv) *stand his rackups*

radge, raj mad, stupid (Carlisle and northern Cumbria)

Raffton Heed Raughton Head

rag[1] hoar frost, rime

rag[2] temper *Ah got me rag out when ah saw him*

rag rugs (see *peg rugs*)

rag-and-bone man collectors of rags, bones and scrap metal in urban areas. They announced their arrival of their horse and cart with a distinctive call. Rags were usually exchanged for *don-* key stones (qv), but by the late 1940s goldfish became the accepted unit of exchange.

raggelt undesirable individual, ill-mannered person (cf *unmenseful*)

raised pie once found on most Lakeland tables at *Kersmas* (qv) time. It was shaped rather like a pork pie, and inside the hard pastry shell was a layer of lean mutton, on top of which was placed a filling of raisins, currants,

A Lakeland raised or 'stannin' pie.

130

Rabbit smoots were ingeniously-designed traps which ensured a plentiful supply of rabbit pies on the table.

peel, cinnamon and brown sugar. This was finished off with a layer of kidney fat and raisins, and over the pie was poured the essential ingredient — a glass (or two) of rum. The pie was then baked for about two hours. (cf *stannin pies*)

rake narrow path along which sheep are driven (possibly from I *reka*, to drive)

ramison long, tedious tale

rammish rank, pungent, sharp, acid (I *rammur*, bitter, pungent)

ramps wild onions

ramscallion, rapscallion rogue, disreputable person

rannel baulk wooden beam positioned across the open hearth in a *fire house* (qv) from which the *rattencrooks* (qv) hung over the fire. Sometimes called the *rannel tree.*

ranty mad

ratch to ransack, to seize meat as a hungry dog does *ratchan' about like a hungry hound.* Also the name used for a thievish, greedy animal

rattencrook, rackencrook implement consisting of an iron rack and a hook for hanging cooking utensils over a fire, hung from the *rannel baulk* (qv) or *fire crane* (qv)

ravel   to entangle; hence *unravel*, to unwind

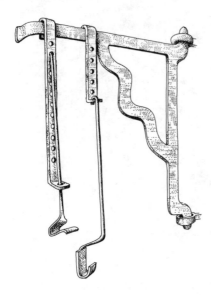

Fire crane and rackencrooks or rattencrooks.

Ravenglass Fair   once held on the Feast of St James the Apostle, the 5th August. It drew people from a wide area, and by the eighteenth century it extended over three days. By the nineteenth century it had become a pale shadow of its former self and was merely a sports meeting, the *St Jam Races*. After a break of ninety years, the fair was revived in 1995.

raw, raa   uncooked; also means cold, as in *it's a raw day*

Rawnsley, Canon H D   Though not a Cumbrian, the name of Hardwicke Drummond Rawnsley (1851–1920) will always be associated with the fells and dales of his adopted region. After working as a lay chaplain in Soho, he was ordained in 1875 and two years later took up the living of Wray, overlooking Windermere, and immediately devoted himself to the preservation of the Lake District environment. He formed the Lake District Defence Society and opposed the Ennerdale Railway scheme. In 1883, as Vicar of Crosthwaite near Keswick, he and his wife Edith founded the Keswick School of Industrial Art, and in 1893 he became one of the founders of the National Trust which, in some respects, is his memorial, but his epitaph was spoken by one of his parishioners — *'Yon's the most active volcano in Europe!'*

reach-tull   hearty invitation to help oneself from the table *Sitha, now, reach-tull an' help thissen* (qv) *to seck* (qv) *as is gaan*

rearing feast   (see *timber raising*)

reasty   rancid, usually applied to bacon

recklin'   weakest of a litter which is usually the last (cf *weedlin'*, *winklin'*, *wrecklin'*) (ON *reklingur*, outcast)

red nettle   stinging red jellyfish (Cartmel)

red-raddle   (see *ruddle*)

reeans, reins   strips of uncultivated land between dales or allotments (ON *rein*, a grassy strip around an arable field)

ree to winnow with a sieve or *riddle* (qv)

reek smoke (see also *needfire*, *rooky*) (I *reykja*, smoke. When Ingolfur Arnarson, the first Norse settler, arrived in Iceland in AD 874 he called the place Reykjavik, the 'bay of smoke' — he mistook the steam from the nearby hot springs for smoke)

reemin' brimful and frothing over

reesty stubborn, obstinate; applied to horses refusing to move

regattas The first Lake District regatta appears to have been held on Windermere in 1775, but the Bassenthwaite regatta of 1779 seems to have established a fashion. The main attraction was the 'swimming sweepstake' — a raft containing several horses was sunk in the middle of Bassenthwaite Lake, and money was placed on which horse swam ashore first. Two years later the first Derwentwater regatta was organised by **Joseph Pocklington** (qv) which, as well as swimming horses, also included a mock sea-battle which delighted hundreds of spectators. The Windermere regattas were, with one or two exceptions, more genteel affairs; in 1825 the 'Admiral of the Lake', Professor John Wilson of Elleray, welcomed future Prime Minister Canning, Walter Scott, William Wordsworth and, according to some reports, Robert Southey.

restle (see *rudstake*)

Richardson, John Born in St John's-in-the-Vale, John Richardson (1817–1886) was a waller, later a schoolmaster and dialect poet. His best-known poem *It's nobbut me* is one of the classics of Cumbrian vernacular poetry.

riddle sieve for corn (see also *ree*)

ridstake (see *rudstake*)

riggin stones stones on the ridge of a building

right as rain excellent, in good condition, in *fine fettle* (qv)

ris, rise[1] brushwood, copse wood (I *hris*, brushwood)

rise[2] growth of wool on a fleece since the last clipping

Ritson, Will The legendary keeper of the inn at Wasdale Head, Will Ritson (1808–1890) boasted that the dale had the highest mountain, the deepest lake and the biggest liar (himself!) in England. His story of crossing his hounds with eagles to produce winged offspring which could outrun any fox, is well known. On another occasion, on a fishing outing to a local tarn with a few guests, the visitors complained they were not getting any bites; Will immediately sent half the party to the other side of the tarn to thrash the water with sticks to drive the fish across to their companions. And, on taking an eminent cleric to the top of Scafell Pike, he announced: *'Tha'll nivver be nearer to Heaven than noo'!*

rive to split, to tear; *slate rivers* are skilled quarrymen who can split a *clog* (qv) of *slate[1]* (qv) into roofing and cladding slates (see also *dressing brake*, *plug-and-feather*, *whittle*) (I *rifa*, N *rive*, to tear, to split)

rivy-rags wasteful person

roak, rowk mist, fog

Robin Goodfellow (see *hob-thrush*)

Robin the Devil also known as Sir Robert Philipson of Langholme (Belle Isle), Windermere. During the Civil War he was besieged on his island by the Parliamentarian, Colonel Briggs. Legend says that in order to exact revenge, he rode into Kendal parish church in pursuit of his enemy, but struck his head on the door and lost his helmet, which can still be seen, hanging high on the north wall. The less romantic interpretation is that the helmet probably belonged to Sir Roger Bellingham.

Robinson, 'Jack' John Robinson was an alderman of the Borough of Appleby and subsequently an MP in Lord North's government. It is said that his name gave rise to the saying *'Afore you can say Jack Robinson'*.

rod fer yer own back said to the parents of pampered children

rogue to cheat, to deal unfairly

'Rogue' Herries one of the most enduring and best-known characters in Cumbrian fiction and the central figure in Hugh Walpole's eponymous novel

roke to scratch

rollock row-lock, the hollow in the gunwale of a small boat into which the oar fits; latterly, an iron u-shaped device to hold the oar

Romney, George (1734–1802) born at Beckside, a small farm near Dalton-in-Furness. After working in his father's joinery workshop, he was apprenticed to Christopher Steele, a Kendal portrait painter. In 1762 he left his wife and two children in Kendal and sought his fortune in London — and did not return home again for thirty-seven years! His portraits — especially those of Lady Hamilton, whom he painted on at least thirty occasions — earned him wealth but little happiness. In declining health, he retreated back to Kendal in 1799, where he was devotedly nursed by the wife he had earlier abandoned. He died in 1802 and is buried in the churchyard at Dalton.

rooky smoky (see *reek*)

roosty rough in manner and attitude

Rosley Fair Until the nineteenth century, Rosley Fair was one of the largest markets for black cattle which were driven south from Scotland. The advent of agricultural auction marts sounded the death-knell for Rosley, and today the Hope and Anchor Inn stands isolated in the middle of the former fairground which once resounded with the noise and bustle of horse dealers, cheap-jacks, mountebanks, *toothpullers* (qv) and *wart charmers* (qv).

ross horse (I *hross*, a horse or mare)

roundheads have no connection with Cromwell and the English Civil War — the name refers to the locally-born inhabitants of the village of Kirkby, overlooking the Duddon Estuary, and is derived from the distinctive 'roundhead' roofing slates produced at the nearby Burlington **slate**[1] (qv) quarries

rowan, roan mountain ash. The rowan tree was sacred to the Norse god Thor and many stories are told of its mystical powers. Cream was stirred with a rowan twig to make the butter come; a sprig of rowan in the *sneck* (qv) of the *byre* door would keep animals safe from the *evil eye* (qv), and visitors to the *Beltane fires* (qv) always carried a branch of rowan to ward

The rowan had mystical powers and was regarded as a charm against the 'evil eye'.

off evil. Legend says that a miraculous revival occured when a coffin carrying the body of a woman bumped into a rowan tree at Boot in Eskdale. The lady revived — but succumbed again shortly after. On her second journey, as the funeral procession neared the tree,

her husband called out to his son: *'Mind! Tek heed o' yon rowan!'* (see *witch-wand*) (ON, I *reynir*, rowan)

rowan tree plough clumsy, cumbersome rowan-tree ploughs were often made in a single day, beginning with the felling of the tree, the seasoning of the wood over a gorse fire, and ending with the fitting of the the iron coulter and sock, probably taken from a previous plough. In the 1850s William Dickinson wrote:
> *Now out wid heam-mead*
> *roan-tree plue*
> *Wid ironin' scanty eneuff,*
> *Lait up strea braffins* (qv),
> *reap traces enue*
> *And see 'at they're o'*
> *draft preuff*

(see also *push plough*)

rowelling insertion of an irritant such as a leather disc, a piece of onion, or a ball of setter grass (*Helleborus foetidus*) into the dewlap of cattle. It was believed that this would allow 'evil humours' to escape from the animal and so improve its condition.

rowky misty, foggy

rub up the wrong way to irritate, to annoy. When the hair of cats and dogs is rubbed upwards, it results in the animal becoming agitated *He rubbed me up the wrong way and no mistake!*

rud stake, restle, ridstake post to which cows are fastened in a *byre* (qv)

ruddle red haematite oxide mixed with grease and used to *smit* (qv) sheep (cf *red raddle*)

rum butter or sweet butter was traditionally given to nursing mothers in the belief that it helped them recover from their confinement. It is still served in china bowls at Cumbrian christenings. This recipe comes from Cartmel:

Melt together half a pound of butter and one pound of soft brown sugar but do not let it boil. Add a little grated nutmeg. Beat it up well and add one tablespoon of rum. When it is beginning to cool, put it in a dish or basin. Serve on crackers

rum butter laiting On the birth or christening of a child, a special bowl of *rum butter* (qv) was traditionally hidden in the house, and this was searched for by groups of young men. After the butter had been found and consumed, the bowl was returned, complete with a monetary offering to the new-born child.

rum do strange, unusual, queer *aye, it's a reet rum do* (cf *queer do*)

rumplement coarse material (see *harden, sark*)

rumshun disturbance, rumpus

runnigate one who runs away from the farm which hired him

rush collapse of a drystone wall, foretold by its *bellying* (qv) *T' dyke's rushed*

rush bark (see *cannel bark*)

rushbearing still carried out at Warcop, Musgrave, Ambleside, Grasmere and Urswick, *rushbearing* is now simply a summer flower festival but originally it had a practical purpose. When burials took place in the nave of the church, the floor was usually beaten earth and sweet-smelling rushes were annually strewn on the floor by parishioners as a boon service. By the early nineteenth century, children in Grasmere undertook this task and were rewarded with a piece of **Grasmere gingerbread** (qv), still baked in the former village school in the

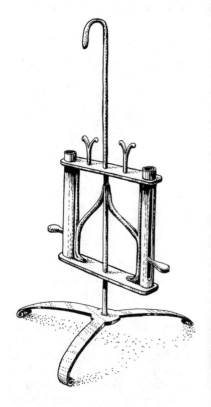

A combined rushstand and candle holder from Townend, Troutbeck.

136

Carrying 'burdens' or 'bearings' at the rushbearing.

corner of the churchyard. (see *bearings*, *marram grass*)

rushlights one of the cheapest forms of illumination. Rushes or sieves (*Juncus conglomeratus*) were cut in late summer, trimmed to about 12–15 inches (30-38cm) long, then peeled, exposing the white, spongy pith. One single strip of green rind was left to support the pith. The peeled rushes were then dipped in bacon fat or mutton fat — the latter was preferred because it contained no salt and therefore gave a clear light which did not sputter. Nothing was wasted — the peelings were made into *bears* (qv). (see *rushstand*)

rushstand, reshstand iron holder used for supporting *rushlights* (qv). It was necessary to hold the *rushlight* at an angle of 45^0 to prevent it dripping or extinguishing the flame. Most *rushstands* were made by local blacksmiths, and there are many designs and patterns. (cf **standarts**)

Russendal Ravenstonedale

russler wrestler

ruttlin', rucklin' a rattling in the throat

ryle, reyle to annoy, to cause vexation *he fair ryled me wi' his noise*

S

sackless useless, helpless (I *saklaus*, simple, innocent, free of blame)

sad firm; unfermented or badly fermented bread is called *sad*

St Bega legendary seventh century Irish saint who landed on the West Cumbrian coast with a small band of nuns intent on founding a religious house. On requesting the local lord for a grant of land, she was summarily dismissed with the jocular assurance that she could have as much land as was covered by snow on Midsummer's Day. The power of prayer — and no doubt the vagaries of the Cumbrian climate — ensured that snow fell on a wide area on that day, so that Bega founded her monastery and gave to Cumbria the name St Bees. **Melvyn Bragg's** (qv) novel *Credo* is based on the Bega legend.

St John Boste (1543?–1594) born at Dufton and at one time was headmaster of Appleby Grammar School. In 1581 he was ordained as a Roman Catholic priest at Rheims, and on returning to England he joined the illegal English Mission, was captured, tried and executed at Durham. He was canonized by Pope Paul VI in 1970 — with the possible exception of **St Patrick** (qv), he is the only true Cumbrian-born saint.

St Cuthbert supposed to have visited Carlisle in AD 685 when he was shown the Roman walls of the city and a fountain still in working order. About this time, King Ecgfrith of Northumbria gave Cuthbert not only the city and the lands within fifteen miles (24km) around it, but also 'Cartmel *et omnes Brittanos cum eo*' — with all the British inhabitants therein.

St Herbert seventh century priest and friend of **St Cuthbert** (qv), who is said to have visited Herbert on the island in Derwentwater which bears his name. According to Bede, the two saints died on the same day, the 20th March AD 687 — Cuthbert on the remote Farne Island and Herbert on his island in Cumbria. By 1374 St Herbert's Island had become a centre of pilgrimage. (see also **hermits**)

St Jam Races (see **Ravenglass Fair**)

139

St John's nut   nut with two kernels (cf *deaf nuts*, *St Mary's nut*)

St Kentigern   or Mungo was a sixth century Bishop of Glasgow and a Celtic saint. According to his thirteenth century biographer, Jocelyn, a Furness Abbey monk, he is supposed to have preached at 'Crosfeld' or Crosthwaite, near Keswick, in or about the year AD 590. The church at Crosthwaite is dedicated to the saint, as are seven others, at Irthington, Grinsdale, Caldbeck, Castle Sowerby, Aspatria, Mungrisdale and Bromfield. The civic coat of arms of the City of Glasgow bears symbols associated with Kentigern — a bush, a bell, a bird and a salmon with a ring in its mouth; the same symbols are to be seen on the iron gates of Crosthwaite Church.

St Mary's nut   nut with three kernels (cf *deaf nuts*, *St John's nut*)

St Ninian   The late fourth and early fifth century Celtic saint, Ninian, the founder of the community at Whithorn, is traditionally said to have preached in Cumbria. However, no definite site has been identified, but place names such as the Ninian well at Loweswater, Ninewells at Brisco near Brampton, and the chapel at Ninekirks, tucked away on the banks of the Eamont near Brougham, all seem to link the saint with Cumbria.

St Patrick   was a Cumbrian, according to some authorities. He is believed to have been the son of a Roman official in one of the West Cumbrian coastal forts. Sometime at the end of the fourth century he was kidnapped and taken as a slave to Ireland, only to return later to his native Cumbria to rekindle the light of Christianity. A good story — but little supporting evidence.

salving   before compulsory dipping of sheep in 1905, animals were often *salved* or smeared with a mixture of rancid butter and Stockholm tar (pron 'sauving')

sammel   hard loamy gravel

Samson's Bratful   collection of prehistoric stone cairns on Stockdale Moor, near Gosforth, supposedly dropped by Satan (later Samson) when the strings on his *brat* or apron snapped

sandscars, sandskers   type of *fluke* (qv) or flat fish similar to a plaice. *Sandscars* have a rough feel when the finger is run from the tail to the head; plaice do not.

sandy   boy's marble of inferior kind (see *taws¹*)

sap whistle   a whistle made from a small branch of a sycamore or willow when the sap is running

sark   a shirt; the term was used mainly in North Cumbria. A *harden sark* (qv) was a shirt made of

A sap whistle.

coarse material, usually hemp or flax; before wearing, it was necessary to wash it and beat it with a *beetlin' stick* (qv) or on a *battlin' steean* (qv), or get the farm boy to wear it for a week or so, a point made by William Dickinson:

> *A carlin' sark, new, was*
> * rumplement* (qv) *gear*
> *To wear next a maisterman's*
> * skin;*
> *So he lent it to t' sarvant to*
> * beatle an' wear*
> *By way of a brekkin' in*

(I *serkur*, OE *serce*, shirt)

sarra   to serve, to feed (animals)

sass   fizzy drink made from the sarsaparilla plant, much favoured by men working in the hot conditions of iron and steel works in Barrow (abbr of sarsaparilla)

savery ducks   form of meatball made from pork. Also known as *ducks wi' veils on*

savin   juniper. *Savin coal* was charcoal made from juniper wood; this produced the finest charcoal and was therefore much prized in the manufacture of gunpowder.

say   shallow dish used to hold water for use in quenching charcoal *pitsteads* (qv)

Scafell   (see Broad Stand)

scale[1]   to disperse, scatter, eg manure

scale[2]   hut or shelter, eg *peat scales* were small huts for storing peat; the word often occurs in place names — North Scale, Bowscale, Seascale etc

scallions   spring onions (OF *eschalogne*, young onion)

scar[1]   cliff, bare rock (I *sker*, a rock,

rocky island)

scar[2]   shoal, stony bed on the foreshore (cf *skeear*)

scarf, scarth   cormorant

scaup   wigeon (cf *bluebill*)

sconce   seat in a recess; *sconce thisen* was an invitation to be seated out of the way. Often the *elding* (qv) and kindling were kept under the sconce, and it was also *a favrit place fer t' dog to lig.* (I *skonsa*, a nook in a house)

scoppy, scop   chaffinch (cf *spink*)

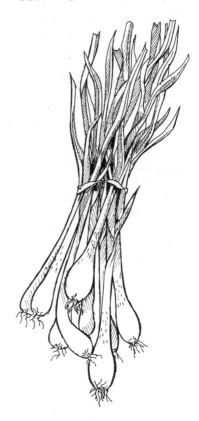

Scallions.

141

scoppy caps schoolboys' peaked caps

scorrock little piece, something of little value

Scot, Michael (?–1291) Possibly born in Cumbria, this eleventh century philosopher, necromancer, astrologer and reputed wizard spent his last years at Holm Cultram Abbey. Educated at Oxford, Paris, Salamanca and Toledo, Michael Scot was skilled in Hebrew, Arabic, chemistry and medicine. For some time he lived in Florence and Padua, and is mentioned by both Boccaccio and Dante. Appointed as astrologer to the Holy Roman Emperor, Frederick II, he was later knighted by Alexander III of Scotland. He died in 1291 and is said to be buried at Holm Cultram — but both Melrose and Glenluce also claim him.

scotchmen Irrespective of their nationality, *scotchmen* were pedlars or itinerant travellers who visited remote farms and hamlets carrying samples of printed cloth, pins, buttons and braids. They usually received a warm welcome not only for their goods but also for the news they carried.

scouse (see *lobscouse*)

scraak screech, as a hen, wildfowl or peacock (I *skraekja*, N *skrike*, to shriek)

scraffel to struggle, to scramble (possibly from ON *skreflas*, to keep one's feet with difficulty)

scram hard rind of bacon or cheese (West Cumbria)

scrams (see *scratchins*) (Wigton)

scran food (Romany word)

scrat to scratch out a meagre living, to be frugal, to scrimp *she's scratted and saved all her life*; also a person who never stops working

scratchins fragments of cooked batter left after fish have been fried in the fish and chip shop. Largely an urban term *a penn'orth a chips and some scratchins, please* (cf *scrams*)

scratlins waste matter from animal fat after melting out the tallow

scrofula (see **King's Evil**)

scroggs rocky ground covered with brushwood

scrood stunted, dwarfed, deformed, defective (see *scrud, taws[1]*)

scrow, scrowe disorder, confusion, untidyness *her house was in sic (qv) a scrowe as thou nivver saw*

scrud a defective marble; inferior and ill-formed (see *scrood, taws[1]*)

scruje up, scrudge up sit closer together *tha mun scruje up an' mak room*

scrunt an apple core

scrunty meagre, stunted, well-worn *yon's a scrunty besom* (qv)

sculling propulsion of a small wooden boat or *punt* (qv) with a single oar at the stern by means of wrist action

scummer long-handled spoon for skimming off the salt meat boiling in cauldrons

scun, skun to throw or hurl something (I *skunda*, to speed, to rush)

scut, skut[1] tailboard of a cart (cf *end board, heck[1]*)

scut, skut² tail of a hare or rabbit

sea pie, sea pyet oystercatcher (cf *cocklemar*)

Sebba Sedbergh

Sebberam Sebergham

seck such (cf *sic, sike*)

seeves, sieves rushes (I *sef*, N *siv*, a rush)

segs¹ hard skin on the palms of the hands and soles of the feet (I *sigg*, thick, hard skin)

segs² small, half-moon shaped nails used to protect the soles and heels of leather shoes

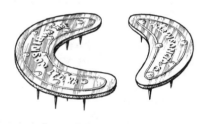

A pair of segs.

self-grey (see *hodden grey*)

sen since, ago *he died six year sen*

sennat seven nights, ie a week

set to arrange the plates and cutlery on a table (cf *lay*)

set on to start *he set me on to work in t' garden*

set pot boiler set or fixed on the fire (OE *settan*, to place)

set-to fight, contest, dispute *a reet set-to*

settle wooden bench having a box below the seat

Sewell, Parson nineteenth century clergyman of Troutbeck about whom many tales are told. On one occasion when preaching in Wythburn Church, his sermon notes fell through a crack between the pulpit and the wall, which resulted in the comment to the congregation: *'T' sarmont's slipt down t' neuk and ah can't git it out, but sitha* (qv) *ah'll read ye a chapter o' t' Bible worth ten on it.'* On another occasion, when asked to pray for fine weather for haymaking, he retorted: *'It's nae use es lang es t' wind's in this quarter!'* Not one to stand on ceremony, he once leaned over the pulpit before Sunday service and enquired of his clerk: *'Hasta* (qv) *seen owt o' two lile sheep o' mine? They're smitten* (qv) *in t' ear like thine, but deeper in t' smit.'* (see also Kirkstone Pass Inn)

Shaking Bottle Sundays Certain Sundays in May were designated as *Shaking Bottle Sundays*. Small pieces of *spanish* (qv) were added to bottles of spring or well water and vigorously shaken to create a drink, *spanish water*. The custom was widespread, from the Penrith area to Kirkby Lonsdale and Kendal, and from Furness to West Cumberland.

shanklings wood used in charcoal burning, usually about three feet (1m) long, which was stacked around the *motty peg* (qv)

sham't embarrassed *'I sham't ut be seen on t' rooads wi' him'*, *Betty Yewdale* (qv) by A C Gibson

sheddins partings made in the fleece of a sheep when *salving* (qv)

sheep band   collar used for tethering the animal; often made of wood

A sheep band.

sheep form, sheep cratch the wooden trestles or benches which support the sheep when it is being *clipped* (qv)

sheep-scoring numerals traditional method of counting sheep, believed to have originated in Celtic times. Although there are variations in the numerals from dale to dale, the one, five, ten, fifteen and twenty remain virtually constant — and are almost identical in Old Welsh, in Cornish, and in the Breton language, emphasising the Celtic connection *(see table below)*.

sheep sime straw rope hung around a sheep's neck and attached to a foreleg to prevent it from leaping fences (cf *cow clog*) (I *sima*, a rope or cord)

shellin' out throwing coins to children at the church gate after a wedding (see *hen silver*); also used used as a euphemism for paying for something *he had to shell out for a new suit*

shelly (see *skelly*)

shelvins, shilvins, skilvins a wooden frame fixed to the top of a cart in order to extend its size and enable larger loads of hay, corn etc to be carried (cf *overins*)

	Coniston	Borrowdale	Old Welsh	Cornish	Breton
1	yan	yan	un	un or onan	unan
2	taen	tyan	dou	deu or dyw	daou
3	tedderte	tethera	tri	try or tyr	tri
4	medderte	methera	petuar	peswar or pedyr	pevar
5	pimp	pimp	pimp	pymp	pemp
6	haata	sethera	chwech	whe	chouech
7	slaata	lethera	sieth	seyth	seiz
8	lowra	hovera	whyth	eath	eiz
9	dowra	dovera	nau	nau	nao
10	dick	dick	dec	dek	dek

A comparison of sheep-counting systems.

shep, shepster the starling (cf *chepster*)

shepherds' guides (see *smit books*)

shepherds' meets annual gathering of shepherds in order to sort out strays. Until 1835, shepherds from **Mardale** (qv), Troutbeck and Kentmere traditionally met on the summit of High Street, where entertainments such as horse racing and Cumberland and Westmorland wrestling took place. Today meets are held in less exposed locations; one of the largest, the Walna Scar Meet, is held in rotation at the Newfield Inn at Seathwaite in Dunnerdale, the Blacksmiths Arms at Broughton Mills, and the Church House Inn at Torver. Horse racing has given way to **hound trailing** (qv) but the day is usually rounded off with a **tatie-pot** (qv) supper.

shift move *shift thissen!* (qv)

shilla, shillies shingle on a beach, gravel

shilvins (see *shelvins*)

shippon, shuppon (see *coo-as*)

shircock mistle thrush (cf *stormie*)

shive, shyve slice of bread or cheese (cf *piece*)

shivver slaty debris, scree

short time working restricted hours *he's bin on short time this month*

shoup, choup seed pod of the wild rose; the term is also found in Scotland

sic such (cf *seck, sike*)

sickle (see *Cumbrian sickle*)

side¹ put away; tidy up *side t' pots fra teable, lass* (see *lay*)

A shep, shepster, chepster or cheppy.

side² airs and graces, snobbishness *he's a big noise i' Lunnon but there's no side on 'im*

sight great many or a quantity *there was a sight o' foak at Rosley Fair*

sike¹ such *'Did ivver ye see sike a pictur?', Betty Yewdale* (qv) by A C Gibson (cf *seck, sic*)

sike² watercourse through wet land; drain (I *siki*, a small stream)

sile¹, syle instrument used for the straining of milk

sile² to strain or to pour liquid through a seive (I *sile*, to strain milk; a term formerly used in E Iceland)

siles naturally-arched cruck timbers around which the pre-seventeenth century Lakeland farmhouses were built (cf *crucks*)

sime, syme straw rope used in thatching stacks etc (I *sima*, a cord or rope)

Simon's Nick deep cleft formed by copper mining in the Coppermines Valley, near Coniston. The legend says that Simon was a German miner of the Company of the Mines Royal who, at the beginning of the seventeenth century, began to work the rich copper seams of the area. Simon, however, was having no luck — until *auld Nick* appeared and offered to show him where the richest deposits were, on condition that Simon sold him his soul. The transaction done, Simon worked happily away mining his seam, until disaster struck and he fell headlong into the cleft he had made. Unlike his escapade at **Devil's Bridge** (qv), Kirkby Lonsdale, this time the Devil had the last laugh ...

sin since

sitha!, sista!, seesta! look!

skarn, sharn, skairn dung (I *skarn*, manure, dung)

skeear cockle-bed (cf *scar²*) (Cartmel)

skelly, shelly freshwater herring found in Ullswater — hence Skelly Neb — Haweswater, Red Tarn on the side of Helvellyn, and in various Scottish lochs

skelp to strike a blow, to chastise, to beat or trash *Ah'll skelp thee!*

skep, skip circular basket made of rushes; also a straw beehive (see *bee boles*) (ON *skeppa*, a basket)

Skiddaw One of Cumbria's best-loved and most-visited mountains was the scene of the most unlikely cavortings on the evening of the 21st August 1815, when the vict-ory of Waterloo was celebrated by a group of local worthies, including Robert Southey, William and Mary **Wordsworth** (qv) with their son John, then aged twelve, James Boswell, the son of Johnson's biographer, Lord and Lady Sunderlin, and a number of somewhat rowdy Keswickians. Southey describes the celebrations:

We roasted beef and boiled plum puddings there; sung 'God Save the King' round the most furious body of flaming tar barrels I ever saw; drank a huge wooden bowl of punch; fired a cannon at every health with three times three, and rolled large balls of tow and turpentine down the steep side of the mountain. The effect was grand beyond imagination ...

Unfortunately, Wordsworth managed to kick over the kettle containing the water brought to dilute the punch; the Keswickians were obliged to drink their rum neat, which resulted in what might, politely, be termed a drunken shambles. The bonfire on Skiddaw to celebrate Queen Elizabeth's silver jubilee was, by all accounts, a much more decorous affair ...

Skiddaw-grey (see *hodden grey*)

Skiddaw Hermit another name for George Smith (cf **Dodd Man**) (see **hermits**)

skilvins (see *shelvins*)

skinch children's truce word, largely used in the north of the county (see *keys*)

skinny mean, stingy; Applied to someone who would *skin a flea for a 'apenny* (see *flea*)

skirl to screech

skoggars outer sleeves worn to protect the arms from grease and dirt, often made from old long woollen stockings with the feet cut off; usually worn when *salving* (qv) sheep

skrike, skreek shriek (I, ON *skraekja*, a shriek)

skut (see *scut)*

slack¹ hollow, depression (I, ON *slakki*, a hollow, boggy place)

slack² coal dust *mend* (qv) *t' fire wi' slack* (Furness, Cartmel and most of Westmorland); small coal (Cumberland)

slack³ little work or business *work's bin slack fer nine month an ah've bin to buroo* (qv)

slampy *fluke* (qv) after spawning when it is white and thin (Cartmel) (I *slaemur*, thin, poor, bad)

slane *peat spade* (qv)

slape slippery *as slape an an eel's tail* (I *sleipur*, slippery)

slape-clogs cheat, one whose word is not to be trusted *he's nobbut a slape-clogs*

slape-finger't butter-fingers; also one guilty of being light-fingered

slashy sloppy, wet weather

slate¹ Lake District slate has been used as a roofing material since the Iron Age. The Romans slated their granaries at Ambleside, Hardknott and elsewhere, and Christopher Wren used **Lakeland slate** for a number of his buildings in London. In the eighteenth century, many local quarries responded to the growing need for slate from the rapidly developing

industrial towns of South Lancashire, and the slate produced ranged in quality fron 'London' (the best) through 'Country', 'Tom' and 'Peg' (the poorest). (see also *bakst'n, clog, closehead quarry, dressing brake, flags, metal, plug-and-feather, trail-barrow, whintin, whittle*)

slate² credit *put it on t' slate*

slatin', slaysteren rebuke *Ah got a reet slaysteren fra gaffer!*

slattery, slatherly showery, wet weather. *It's slating down* means it is raining heavily. (ON, I *sletta*, to bespatter)

sleck trough water trough in which a blacksmith slakes or cools his iron work

Slee, Lanty (1802–1878) a notorious though much admired distiller of illicit whisky from potatoes. The remains of his stills may yet be seen on the fellsides and in ancient quarries around Little Langdale. His whisky sold for about ten shillings a gallon, yet he made sufficient money to buy Greenbank Farm in Little Langdale where he died in 1878 aged seventy-six. It is said that Lanty sold his whisky, reputed to be the best in the district, to the magistrates who on several occasions convicted him! (see also *'cow and worm'*)

slemp sly (ON *sleyma*, a scamp)

sling depart, go away *Sling tha' hook!*

slocken to quench thirst or fire (see *sleck trough*)

slopst'n shallow stone or earthenware sink

smatch smattering

smit[1] a mark or sign

smit[2] to smear or mark, as with sheep (I *smyrja*, OE *smittan*, to smear or anoint)

smit books Sometimes called *shepherds' guides*, these books were first introduced in 1817 by a Martindale farmer, Joseph Walker. Each farm was represented by two fierce-looking sheep, one showing the appropriate *lug marks* (qv), the other the *smit marks* (qv). The idea was successful and several editions were produced, and well-thumbed copies can still be found on farmhouse mantelshelves. The latest edition, by G F Brown and W Rawling, was published in 1985.

in Borrowdale, graphite from the Seathwaite mine was used until the 1830s. There are over 700 *smit marks* currently in use in Cumbria. (see *ruddle*, *smit books*, *wad*)

Smith, George (c1825–1876) the Skiddaw Hermit (see **hermits**)

smittal, smittle infectious, contagious (N *smittsom*, contagious)

smoot, smout, smute the run of a hare or other animal through a fence or wall (see *rabbit smoot*); a narrow passage or hole (cf *snicket*) (N *smau*, a narrow passage; ON, I *smuga*, a hole)

smuggling The Solway and Irish Sea coasts of Cumbria afforded fertile ground for the 'running trade', especially in the eighteenth

An illustration from a Lakeland smit book.

smit marks the mark on the fleece of a sheep to indicate ownership. Now made with dye, in the seventeenth, eighteenth and nineteenth centuries *rud balls* of haematite iron oxide were used;

century. From Millom to Bowness the coast was relatively sparsely-populated and badly-patrolled. Small sailing ships could reach Ireland, Scotland and the Isle of Man — where the lower rates of

A 'sneck posset' could be a traumatic experience.

149

customs duty applied — in a matter of hours, returning with contraband cargoes. The Isle of Man featured prominently in this trade. In 1724 a report claims that 'the town [Whitehaven] and country were mostly supplied with brandy, rum, tea, tobacco, soap … from that "Warehouse of Frauds" [ie the Isle of Man]'. The 'trade' declined after the Revestment Act of 1765, when the British Parliament took control of the Manx customs and paid the Lord of Man, the Duke of Atholl, £70,000 in compensation. This gave rise to the rhyme:

> *Ah! babes unborn will lament*
> *   the day*
> *When the Isle of Man was*
> *   sold away*
> *And every Old Wife who loves*
> *   her dram*
> *Will bewail the loss of the Isle*
> *   of Man*

smute (see *smout*)

snape to check or restrain growth (of plants)

sneck latch of a door or gate

sneck drawer covetous person

sneck posset to have the door closed in one's face, figuratively and literally. Often applied to suitors who were not welcome.

sneckin' up t' yat The children of a village would *sneck up t' yat* (fasten the church gate) just as the newly-married couple were about to emerge from the ceremony. They could be persuaded to re-open the gates only when the bridegroom *shelled out* (ie threw handfuls of coins to the

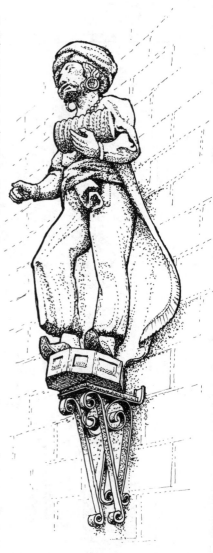

The sign of the snuff maker, Lowther Street, Kendal.

crowd). The custom still prevails in several parts of Cumbria. (see *hen silver*)

snevil snail

snicket narrow passage between buildings (see *smoot*)

snig[1] small eel

snig[2] to haul, to drag out, especially timber from woodland

snirp, snirrup to shrivel (with cold, heat, drought etc); also to turn up one's nose *she snirp't up her neb* (qv) *at me*

snitch[1] nose

snitch[2] to inform, to tell tales

snod smooth, sleak, neat (ON *snodinn*, made smooth)

snoot bands iron or brass plates on the *neb* (qv) of **clogs** (qv) (cf *caulkers*)

snuff once made in Whitehaven, Penrith and Kendal, where the first water-powered mill was opened on Natland Beck in 1740. The tobacco was brought by packhorse trains from Whitehaven over the Hardknott and Wrynose passes, and also from Lancaster. Today the production is concentrated in the Kendal area, though the Aynam mill was destroyed by fire in 1983.

Solway Moss a mile or so northeast of Gretna — but just within Cumbria. This flat area, about seven miles (11km) in circumference, is a huge raised bog composed of mud and fibrous material, covered by a relatively dry crust which supports mosses, rushes and silver birch scrub. In the winter of 1771, after heavy rain, the bog burst on the east side, inundating some 500 acres (200ha) of farmland to a depth of thirty feet (9m). More than thirty families lost their houses and were made destitute.

sonks green-turf sods used as substitute saddles

soople business end of a *flail* (qv) (see *swingle*)

sop body of iron ore or *black lead* (qv) *in situ*

sops (see *buttered sops*)

sotter to boil slowly, to simmer; the sound emitted in boiling any thick substance such as oatmeal porridge

sour dockin common sorrel

souse something very sour such as brine or sour whey

souse tub vessel holding brine or sour whey used for pickling meat

souted diseased (especially sheep)

Souther Fell phantom army A well-documented apparition, first recorded in 1735 when a servant employed by William Lancaster of Blakehills, about half a mile from Souther Fell, saw a great phantom army on the east side of the fell. It was seen again by William Lancaster and others in 1737, and again on Midsummer Eve 1745 when twenty-six people witnessed the 'army'. Mass delusion or optical illusion? (see also *Brocken spectre*)

souty ailing pig or sheep

sowen extremely *a sowen girt chap*

sowens husks of oatmeal were steeped in water and the resulting residue was served up boiled in milk; this was known as *sowens*:
    Oh! for Westmorland sowens
      and cream

spanish liquorice, so-called because of its country of origin. The roots of the plant were commonly chewed by children, but the concentrated black liquorice was put in bottles with spring water and made into a drink. (see *Shaking Bottle Sundays*)

sparrables small nails used by shoemakers

spas (see **holy wells and spas**)

spean to wean lambs etc (I *speni*, animal teat)

Spedding, Carlisle A man of great ability, Carlisle Spedding (1695–1755) managed Sir James Lowther's coalmines at Whitehaven in the eighteenth century. As well as inventing the *steel mill* (qv) to illuminate the mines, he also developed a system of ventilation known as 'coursing the air'. Both innovations enabled pits to be driven to deeper depths and more coal to be won. His greatest achievement was the sinking of the Saltom Pit between 1730 and 1731; undoubtedly the most remarkable coal mine of its day, it reached an unprecedented depth of 456 feet (139m) and was the first to mine coal beneath the Irish Sea. Carlisle Spedding was killed in a mining accident in 1755, but his work was continued by his son, James.

Speeatry Aspatria; '*Speeatry, lowp oot*' (porter at Aspatria Station) means 'This is Aspatria, kindly leave the train'

spelk, speel, spell[1] small splinter of wood; also a rod to fasten down thatch. A *spelk basket* is one made from shavings of oak laths. (see *swill*) (I *spelkur*, a shaving of wood)

spell[2] spring trap used in the game of *knur and spell* (qv)

spice cupboard small, square recess near to the fire in which spices and salt were kept. Often these cupboards had beautifully carved oak doors bearing the initials of the farmer and his wife, and the date.

spink chaffinch (cf *scoppy*)

spinning galleries Open galleries on the exteriors of farms and barns where, it is argued, the spinning of wool took place. The name, however, is misleading; certainly spinning was one activity undertaken, but others, such as the storing and preparation of fleeces, wool, yarn and cloth, were also important. Of the forty or so galleries listed in Cumbria, the majority face north or east. It is argued that in many cases the wool room for storage of fleeces lay behind the gallery; at *clipping time* (qv), the sheep were clipped in the shade, the work being arduous and sweaty, then the fleeces were thrown up to a helper standing on the gallery and put at once into the store room. Galleries also served a social function, as Adam Sedgwick noted at Dent:

The galleries were places of mirth and glee and active, happy industry for here might be heard the buzz of the spinning wheel and the hum and the songs of those who were carrying out the labours of the day

A spice cupboard door from Longsleddale.

Some of the best examples may be seen at Yew Tree Farm, Coniston, Thorn House, Hartsop, and Hodge Hill, Cartmel Fell.

spitten image strong likeness *yon barn's* (qv) *his fadder's spitten image*

spittin' slight shower of rain

spouse small *flukes* (qv) or other fish (cf *chatterment*) (Cartmel)

spring clogs clogs (qv) having wooden soles in two pieces which are hinged under the instep with leather

sprint stick and noose snare for catching birds (see also *geldert*)

153

So-called 'spinning galleries' were used for a wide variety of activities associated with the woollen industry.

sproag, sprogue to ramble about for pleasure

sprod young salmon or salmon trout

sprog[1] to stop a wheel by inserting a chock betwen the spokes

sprog[2] anything used to *sprog* wheels

stag colt or young horse

Stagg, John 'The Blind Bard of Cumberland' (1770-1823) lost his sight when a child, but became a poet and collector of folktales and songs, as well as an accomplished fiddler. (see *fiddlers*)

stand kurn (see *kurn*)

standarts adjustable candle and *rushlight* (qv) holders which stood on the ground (cf *rushstand*)

stang[1] cart shaft (cf *limmers*) (N *stang*, I *stöng*, a post or pole)

stang[2] to sting *t' cleg's* (qv) *stang't me*

stang riding method of publicly shaming a supposed guilty party; usually reserved for adultery or wife-beating — but occasionally for husband-beating. A man or woman, dressed as or impersonating the victim, was paraded around to each house on a *stang*[1] (qv) or plank, stops being made while the 'rider' proclaimed in doggerel why he or she was being humiliated — the last stop being outside the victim's home.
For wife-beating:
> *It isn't for my part 'at I ride this stang*
> *'Tis for Johnny Johnson 'at has done wrang*

For husband-beating:
> *Ting tang to the sign of the pan!*

> *Our good neighbour's wife*
> *She has beat her good man*

stangers ironwork (hangings) to a gate or door (see *hing-ins*)

stank pool, artificial pond

stannin pies (see *raised pies*)

starved suffering from cold *Ah'm starved to death* (OE *steorfan*, to die, to suffer intensely)

statesmen derived from 'estatesmen', that group of independent yeomen farmers who formed a kind of rural middle class, neither gentry nor hired farmhands. They held their land by customary tenure rather than by copyhold, and until the union of the Scottish and English crowns they were obliged to take up arms in any Border warfare.

Steadman, George Of all the heroic figures in the annals of Cumberland and Westmorland wrestling (qv), George Steadman (1846–1904), of Asby near Appleby, has no equal. In 1900 at the age of fifty-four this gentle giant, with the appearance of an avuncular bishop, quit the ring, having won the championship at Grasmere on no fewer than seventeen occasions.

stee, stey ladder; hence Sty Head Pass (I *stigi*, a ladder, *stigur*, a steep path)

steel mill Developed in 1730 by **Carlisle Spedding** (qv), this hand-cranked geared wheel turned a steel disc against which a piece of flint was held. This gave off a stream of sparks which, it was believed, would be less likely to ignite methane gas in Cumbrian coalmines. The implement was operated by children of eight years of age; it continued in use until the invention of the Davy safety lamp in 1819. Primitive though it was, it allowed mines to go deeper and so enabled more coal to be won.

steepin' rain   heavy, penetrating rain

Steevla   Staveley

steg   gander or young game-cock (ON *steggi*, a male bird)

steg or stag mains   cockfighting (qv) competitions for young cocks

stick-a-roger   boys' game once common in Low Furness; a variation of *montikitty* (qv) played in the Wigton area

sticks   (see *crooks*)

stiddy, studdy   anvil (I *steðji*, an anvil)

A stiddy.

stinkin' Roger   knotted figwort

stirk   young bullock or heifer, usually one to two years old

stirrup oil, strap oil   chastisement given to a child with a leather belt

stoat   fed up, tired *Ah's reet stoat*

stonecrop   plant often found growing in the walls of Lakeland

cottages since, traditionally, it supposedly protected the house from lightning

stopping on   At the end of a six month hiring, farm servants could choose to *stop on* or offer themselves for hire in the various **hiring fairs** (qv) at Whitsun or Martinmas.

stormie, stormcock   mistle thrush (cf *shircock*)

stouk   group of sheaves of corn

stoup   (see *gate stoup*)

stour, stoor   dust

> *And the queer old men that*
> *   walked about*
> *In the livery of the poor*
> *And trailed a cart, like burden*
> *   beasts*
> *To gather filth and stour ...'*

A Dream of Steam, Henry H Davies (1842)

streek, straik   to *lay out* (qv) a corpse. The *streekin'* was usually followed by tea-drinking and a *crack* (qv) (see *coze house*, *wake*)

streemers   Northern Lights, or aurora borealis (cf *Lord Derwentwater's Lights*, *merry-dancers*)

strickle   instrument for sharpening scythes made by pitting a block of wood with tiny depressions, then smearing it with tallow and finally sprinkling sharp quartz sand from the shores of the nearest tarn onto the fat (OE *stricel*, a whetstone)

strinkle   to sprinkle, to scatter about

sturdy, stordy   sheep disease spread by dogs and foxes which have tapeworms. The parasite's eggs are laid in that part of the brain which controls the sight; the sheep becomes blind in one eye, wanders in circles and loses condition. It was cured by trepanning the animal — usually at full moon when, it was believed, the skull was softer. (OF *étourdi*, giddy)

stye, styne, styan painful gathering on the eyelid, traditionally cured by rubbing lightly with a gold wedding ring

Swaddles, Swarddles Swaledale sheep; used as the logo for the Yorkshire Dales National Park, part of which is in Cumbria (cf *Herdwick, Teeswatter*)

swael, sweel to burn unsteadily, to flare up (I *svaela*, heat accompanied by thick smoke)

swammel, swarmel to climb a pole, rope or tree by grasping it with the arms and knees

swankin' strong, lusty, anything very large; also boastful *she's swankin' about her new coat*

swanky small beer or weak ale

A Swaddle.

The swiller's mare, a foot-operated vice, was used in the making of 'swill baskets'.

sward, swath, swarth bacon rind (see *scram*)

swatch sample or pattern

sweet butter (see *rum butter*)

sweet mart pine marten, now a very rare species (see *foomart*)

swill oval basket woven from oak laths or *spelks* (qv). Once an important industry in Lakeland woodlands, *swills* were used wherever a hard-wearing container was required. Today one or two *swillers* — including one woman — still practise the craft. (see also *taws¹*)

swiller's mare foot-operated vice and seat used by *swill* (qv) basket makers

swingle instrument for beating hemp; the swinging part of a *flail* (qv)

syke small stream

syle (see *sile¹*)

syling pouring down, *teeming* (qv) down *it's fair syling down*

T

t' abridged version of the definite article. An excellent example is to be found on the walls of Hawkshead Church where a scriptural text, painted in 1711 by William Mackreth, reads:

In the begining [sic] *was the Word and the Word was with God, and t' word was God.* John 1:i

Is this a touch of the vernacular — or did Mackreth simply run out of space?

ta (see *teh*)

ta year this year

tack peculiar flavour or taste

taestral, taistrel violent, mischievous person (see also *taggelt*)

taffy join ostensibly a social gathering where toffee was made in a pan, but in effect these gatherings became match-making exercises when desperate mothers attempted to get their daughters attached to eligible bachelors

taggelt a useless, disreputable person; a term of contempt *he's nobbit a girt drunken taggelt!* (see also *taestral*)

Taggy bell eight o'clock curfew bell still rung on the old tenor bell of Kirkby Stephen Church

tait small fluff on woollen clothes

tak to take *it'll tak him o' his time t' git t' Carel* (qv) (cf *tek*) (I *taka*, to take)

tak up to improve *it's spittin'* (qv) *but happen it'll soon tak up*

Tally Ho! Tally Ho! Follow the Hounds foxhunting (qv) song second only to *D' ye ken John Peel?* (qv)

tangel, tangle, tanggal seaweed. On the Cumbrian coasts, some farms had *tangle dales* allocated, from which seaweed was harvested for use as a manure. (I *thang*, seaweed)

tannin' a smacking; often used as an admonition to a naughty child *Ah'll tan thy backside!* (cf *ledderin'*)

tar costrel small bucket containing Stockholm tar; used at *clippin' time* (qv)

tar machine The smell of molten tar was believed to cure **whooping cough** (qv) and children were often taken to breathe in the fumes when roads were being repaired. And, in the author's experience, it worked!

tar plaster plaster made from Stockholm tar (the resin from pine trees); used on animals for slight cuts and wounds

tarrant a badly-behaved person or child

tatie-pot *Herdwick* (qv) mutton, if properly cooked, can quite literally be a royal feast. It was served at the coronation banquet of Queen Elizabeth II in 1953, and more recently when she visited High Yewdale Farm, Coniston. But to savour it to the full it is best in a *tatie-pot*; no *merry neet* (qv), *hunt supper* or *shepherds' meet* (qv) would be complete without this most traditional dish. Consisting of *Herdwick* mutton, black pudding and onions topped with

A tar costrel and sheep marker were used at 'clippin' time'.

crisp brown potatoes, and accompanied by pickled onions and a *laal bit o' red cabbish*, the Lancashire hot-pot pales into insignificance ...

tatie-puddin' potatoes and groats boiled in a *puddin' poke* (qv) in broth or soup

taties-an'-point meagre diet. William Dickinson suggests that the phrase is derived from the habit in poor households of placing a meagre piece of butter or bacon fat on the table; the diners loaded their spoons with potatoes and were allowed to point towards the morsel but not touch it! (see *bread and scrape*)

taws[1] marbles. Sadly the once ubiquitous playground game has almost died out. The marbles had various names such as *potties* (qv), *stonies*, *flinties*, *glassies*, *alleys* (qv) and *blood alleys* (those streaked with red). Inferior kinds were *sandies* and *scruds* (qv). *Bobbers* were large marbles which were pitched or bowled. (see also *cruddy, dobbers, don, donnocks*)

taws[2] oak *laths* (qv) running lengthways down a *swill* (qv) basket

teanal cockle basket (see also *coul, cramb, hardbacks, jumbo, skeear, wheaat*)

teem to pour out, to empty; to rain heavily *it's teeming down*. In the north-east of Cumbria *pour* is used. (cf *syling*) (I *taema*, to empty)

teensel brushwood used for repairing hedges (ancient Furness term)

Teeswatters Cumbrian term for the breed of sheep indigenous to Teesdale (cf *Herdwick, Swaddles*)

teh, ta you *Hoo 's teh gitten on?* (cf *tha*)

tek take *tek heed, mind* (cf *tak*)

telling the bees An obscure custom in which, after a death in a family, a person was appointed to lay his or her hands on the bee *skep* (qv) and tell the bees who had died. Sometimes the hive was decorated with black ribbon and occasionally crumbs from the funeral feast (see *arval*) were left out for the bees. The custom prevailed in various places, including Ireland, Scandinavia and Cumbria, where it was still respected as late as the 1950s.

telt told *Ah telt 'im nut to gang* (qv)

teng to sting *Ah gat teng'd wi' a wamp* (qv) (OE *stingan*, to sting)

tenter frames hooked wooden frames (later made of iron) on which woollen cloth was dried and stretched, hence the term *on tenter hooks* (OF *tendre*, to stretch)

term, tierm, tearm half-yearly holiday for the hirings at Martinmas and Whitsun

Taws, once highly-prized schoolboy possessions.

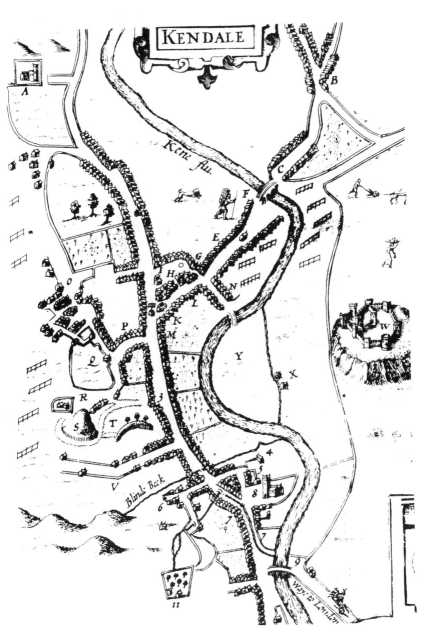

John Speed's map of Kendal from 1610 shows tenter frames on both sides of the River Kent.

terrible excellent, first-rate. A hound can be a *terrible good runner*, a **wrestler** (qv) may be a *terrible rustler*, and of course the ladies of Dent were *terrible knitters* (see below).

Terrible Knitters of Dent were neither inept at their craft or frightening to behold, since the adjective here means excellent *(see above)*. The phrase was used by Robert Southey in 1834.

teufat, tewet, tewit lapwing

teyk (see *tike*)

tha, thi you, your (cf *teh*)

thar' cakes, tharth cakes thick oat or barley cakes cooked among the embers of the fire. The name could be derived from 'hearth', or it may come from the OE *theorf*, meaning unleaven.

that so *Ah'm that glad tha's come!*

theatres The tradition of folk theatre goes back at least to the *play-jiggs* of the seventeenth century (see **Hoggart, Thomas**), but by the eighteenth century, groups of travelling 'barn-stormers' were performing in stables and barns throughout Cumbria. Whitehaven acquired a purpose-built theatre in Roper Street in 1769, Ulverston began building its Theatre Royal in 1796 and Carlisle opened its theatre in Blackfriars Street in 1813. The repertoire was catholic, and included such luminaries as Mr Saxoni, who 'exerted himself in a peculiar manner by a novel display of activity on the tightrope', musical farces, comic songs and Shakespearian tragedies —

often all on the same bill. William Fleming, the Pennington diarist, attended a performance of *The Tragedy of Barnwell* in Ulverston in November 1800 — but found the audience more entertaining than the actors, including 'a lady in the boxes [who] was the only person I saw affected so much as to shed a tear — and from certain circumstances in her behaviour this evening, I am induced to suspect brandy rather than the sympathetic proofs of sensibility'. (see **Deans, Mrs Charlotte**)

thek, thak thatch, but originally the term was applied to any roof covering (OE *thaec*, I *thak*, thatch)

thi (see *tha*)

thible (see *thivel*)

thick to be in league with *they're as thick as thieves* (I *thekkja*, to know, to be acquainted with)

thimmel pie blow to the head with the thimble on a woman's finger; reprimand for children

thingmount Behind Fell Foot Farm in Little Langdale is a square, terraced mound similar to Tynwald Hill in the Isle of Man. It is believed to be a *law-ting* or law hill of the Norse-Irish settlers, where the laws were read out and justice was seen to be done. 'This thingmount in Little Langdale may be regarded as the Lakeland Tynwald', W G Collingwood.

think on! admonition to remember *Think on! Tha mun cum wi' brass* (qv) (cf *mind¹*) (central Cumbria)

Thirlmere apparition Harriet Martineau relates the story of a

murdered bride who was drowned in Thirlmere, and who then returned to her wedding feast at Armboth Hall. Bells were heard to ring, plates and dishes clattered, and the table was spread by unseen hands. And at the same moment a large, ghostly dog was seen to swim across the lake ... Present-day 'ghost-busters' should be warned that the site of the house was destroyed when the Thirlmere reservoir was created.

thissen yourself

thivel, thible wooden implement for stirring, especially porridge (ON *thyvel*, porridge stick)

thoft seat in a boat (Cartmel) (I *thófta*, an oarsman's seat in a boat)

thought on esteemed *he's highly thought on*

thrang busy *as thrang as Throp's wife; we're as thrang as can be wi' t' clippin*

threap, threep to dispute noisily, to argue persistently (OE *threapian*, ON, I *threfa*, to argue, to grumble)

Three Shires Stone Both Christopher Saxton's map of Cumberland and Westmorland (1576) and John Speed's map of Cumberland (1610) mark 'shire stones upon Wrenose' where, before 1974, Cumberland, Westmorland and Lancashire met at the summit of the pass. In 1671 there were three stones, one in each of the three counties, but today the spot is marked by a single limestone pillar with 'Lancashire' on one side and WF 1816 on another. The

A thible or thivel for stirring porridge.

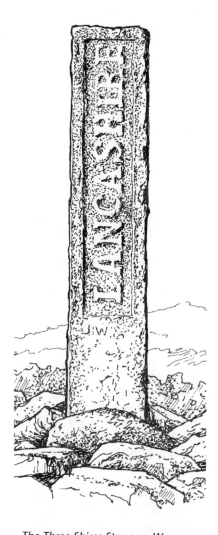

The Three Shires Stone on Wrynose Pass once marked the junction of the county boundaries of Cumberland, Westmorland and Lancashire.

initials are those of William Field of Cartmel, who had the stone carved in 1816, but it was not erected here until after his death in 1860.

Threlkat Threlkeld

threshwood baulk of timber laid across the entrance to a farm to prevent rainwater entering the *hallan* (qv). Often nailed to the threshwood were either two crossed straws or a horseshoe to keep away the *evil eye* (qv).

thrinter (see *thrunter*)

thropple throat, windpipe

throstle song thrush

Throstle's Nest another name for Wigton. It is said to be derived from an exclamation uttered by an exile who, returning from London, stood on Howrigg Bank and cried *'The Throstle's Nest of all England!'* Wigtonians are sometimes known as *throstles*.

throughs stones which help to tie the two faces of a **drystone wall** (qv) together. They often project through the wall on each side — hence the name. (see also *cams, heartings, footings*)

throwing the stocking somewhat boisterous event at eighteenth and early nineteenth century weddings. The newly-married couple sat in bed, while the men tried to hit the groom and the women attempted to hit the bride by throwing the bride's stockings over their shoulders. Those who were successful were assured that their own marriage was near. (see *bidden wedding, bridecake, sneckin' up t' yat*)

Throwing the stocking, a Cumbrian wedding custom.

Tom Skelton, the fool of Muncaster Castle, who gave his name to 'tomfoolery'.

168

thrumwort water plantain

thrunter, thrinter, trinter a three-year old sheep, literally a sheep of three winters (see *twinter*) (I *threvetur*, three years old)

thunner-stanes quartz pebbles in becks, thought to be produced by thunder; erratic boulders

thwaet, thwaite a clearing (ON *tveit*, a piece of land which has been enclosed)

tide-wreck line of seaweed and flotsam left at high tide

tidy in a good state *'Hoo's ta blowing?' 'Oh, tidy fer an auld 'un'*

tierm (see *term*)

tift to pant, to puff and blow

tig to touch lightly; a children's game

tight drunk *as tight as wax* (cf *addled, fluz'd, in liquor, kalied, kettelt*)

tike, tyke, teyk dog; also applied to an odd person. Formerly used as a term of abuse, it is said that a Curwen of Workington Hall shot a Howard of Corby in a duel at the Sands, Carlisle, for offensively using the word *tike* when addressing him. (ON *tik*, a bitch)

till to *Ista gaan till t' market?* (I, AS *til*, to)

timber raising when a house or barn was nearing completion, the owner would invite his neighbours to help him erect the roof. They would be rewarded with a *merry neet* (qv) held in the newly finished building. (see also *boon ploughing, clay daubin*)

time period of an apprenticeship; *out of his time* means that the apprenticeship has been served and the young man is now a craftsman (see also *lowznin'*)

tin can lurky somewhat noisy children's game in which the one who is 'it' seeks out another player in hiding, and then races him or her to be the first to kick a tin can (Furness) (cf *tipwhip*)

tip (see *tup*)

tipwhip (see *tin can lurky*) (Workington)

tite soon *Ah'd as tite do it as nut*

titter sooner, quicker (ON *titt*, soon)

> *For t' time flang by at sic a reate,*
> *Titter nor wings o' birds*
> *Shifting Scenes*, J Stanyan Bigg

tittermest nearest, soonest

tod fox

toitle to topple, cause to fall down

tom beedel cockchafer

tomfoolery said to refer to the sixteenth century resident fool at Muncaster Castle, Tom Skelton. The full-length portrait in the castle shows him dressed in a green, white and yellow gown, carrying a hat, staff and bowl.

tom spade large spade with a long cross-handle, used for cutting drains in upland areas

tommy food served to hired farmhands by the farmer's wife; *what sort o' tommy-shop is it?* was an important question asked at the *hirings* (qv)

toothache, cures for Many eighteenth and nineteenth century toothache cures depended for their potency on a mixture of ether, laudanum and camphor,

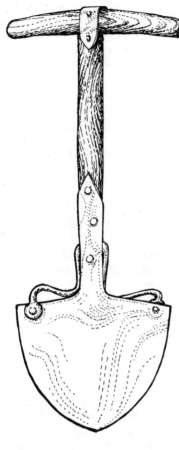

Tom spades were used for cutting drains.

but others depended on the powers of folk medicine. At Hawkshead a hollow tooth-stopping made of a splinter of wood from the remains of the ancient gibbet was much respected, and to improve the teeth of a child it was recommended to rub them with 'the brains of

a hen or let a horse breathe into the child's mouth twice a day which may prevent convulsive fits'. (see **folk cures, toothpullers**)

toothpullers For sufferers who had exhausted the usual folk remedies (see **toothache, cures for**) help was at hand during the hiring fairs (qv) when *toothpullers* plied their art. The patient sat in a chair on a makeshift stage in front a fascinated crowd of onlookers while his or her teeth were extracted — but always accompanied at the side by a small brass band which would strike up to disguise any distress signals the patient might emit.

top to snuff a candle

toppins, toppin peats sods of coarse grass, dried and used for fuel

torfel, torfer to die, to decline in health

Tosspot character in the *pace egg song* (qv)

touching the corpse Until the nineteenth century it was usual for mourners to view the corpse and to touch it. This custom was derived from an ancient belief that if the murderer touched the body of his victim it would bleed; consequently, mourners had to pass this test to indicate that they were not responsible for the death. (see *coze house, streek*)

trail-barrow heavy wooden sled used by quarrymen to transport slate[1] (qv) down steep fellsides. The sled had two *stangs* (qv), between which a man was placed, taking the position of a draught

Trail-barrows were used to transport slate down steep fellsides.

animal. On scree slopes he then ran down the loose shale, being carried forward by the weight of a quarter of a ton of slate behind him. Having unloaded the slate, the trail-barrow had to be taken back up the slope. One Joseph Clarke of Seathwaite in Borrowdale sledged five tons of slate in a single day from the Honister slate quarries, travelling over seventeen miles (27km). This method of transportation ceased at Honister in 1881.

trail hounds (see *hound trailing*)

trantelments odds and ends, useless trifles

trapesin', traipsin' walking about without a purpose, sauntering *he's allus trapesin' aboot*

treading for fluke method of catching *flukes* (qv). With bare feet, participants follow the ebb tide, carefully feeling for the fish. There is no mistaking a 'catch'. (see *clockermunje*)

Trepena Torpenhow

trig tight-fitting, snug *these shoon are as trig as skin*

trinter (see *thrunter*)

trivet iron tripod for supporting pans on the fire (cf *brandreth*)

trod track or beaten way, footpath (ON *trodd*, OE *trod*, a track, path)

trollops dirty, disreputable person

Troughton, Edward (c1753–1835) born at Wellcome Nook near Corney, south-west Cumbria. He became one of the most celebrated astronomical instrument makers of his day, making telescopes for Greenwich Observatory, and supplying compasses and theodolites for many surveying expeditions. His work earned him the coveted Copley medal of the Royal Society. He is buried in Kensal Green cemetery, London.

trounce[1] long, weary journey *we had a bonny trounce afore we gat yam* (qv)

trounce[2] to whip, to punish

Troutbeck giant (see **Hird, Hugh**)

Troutbeck hundreds At the beginning of the seventeenth century, the pastures of Troutbeck (Westmorland) were divided into three divisions or **hundreds**, the Highest, the Middle, and the Lowest. Each had a constable, a carrier and a bull, which resulted in the oft-repeated rhyme:

Three hundred carriers,
Three hundred bulls,
Three hundred constables
And several hundred fools

Troutbeck Mayor Hunt (see *mayor hunts*)

trunlins sheep or rabbit droppings

tudder the other

tumble-tom form of haysweep

tummel cars primitive single-horse, two-wheeled carts made entirely of wood. The wheels were usually *clog wheels* (qv) which turned with the axle underneath the body of the cart.

tummelt to tumble, to fall down (N *tumle*, tumble, topple)

tummins rough cardings of wool

tup, tip ram, male sheep. The Eskdale Tup Show, usually held on the last Friday in September, was a social occasion when farmers cast experienced eyes over the stock, and *tups* were hired out for breeding purposes. (see also *wether*)

tupping time takes place in November, when the *tups* (rams) are mated with the *yowes* (ewes) to ensure lambing in the following spring

turbary peat moss

turn sudden affliction or illness *she's had a nasty turn*

turned off discharged from service, dismissed

turnip bread form of bread in which flour is adulterated with boiled turnips in order to stretch the available grain supply. William Fleming, a Furness yeoman

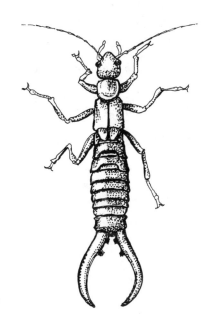

A twitchbell.

farmer, recorded in his diary in August 1801:

To make turnip bread, take off the skins from your turnips and boil them till soft; bruise them well and press out the juice; add an equal weight of wheat flour and knead them up with a sufficient quantity of salt and bake them. The great scarcity of wheat flour, oatmeal and potatoes, and the consequent high prices, induced many families to make bread according to this recipe in 1800.

turnip lanterns turnips hollowed out and made into a grotesque face, which were then lit with the stump of a candle. Often made

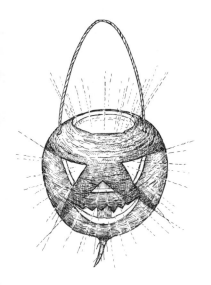

A turnip lantern.

for Hallowe'en but also on the 5th November.

twa　two; *Nowt's* (qv) *a secret after twa knows it* is a Cumbrian saying

twang　distinctive accent or intonation of the voice *Ah cud tell by his twang he weren't fra' Forness Fells*

Twelfth Night　(see *Brough Holly Night*)

twine[1]　to fret, to whine

twine[2]　to twist　*twine syme* (qv) *round yon rowan*

twinter　two year old sheep, literally, a sheep of two winters (cf *thrunter*)

twitchbell　earwig

tyadds　toads (see *paddock*)

tyke　(see *tike*)

tyreing platform　iron plate which secured wooden cartwheels during hooping. The iron tyre or rim was heated until red-hot, dropped over the wheel, and immediately dowsed with water so that it contracted on the *fellies* (qv).

U

uggery welt form of cricket played in Aspatria. The bats were shortened pick-shafts and the *cat* or ball was a piece of wood 3 or 4 inches (7.5–10cm) long.

unbethowt remembered

unbiddable obstinate, recalcitrant

under under the care of the doctor *Ah've been under the doctor wi' me leg fer three months*

undermer lower, under

unext uninvited

unfewsom awkward, unbecoming

ungaan ready to depart, not gone yet; *just ungaan* means on the point of death

unkent unknown

unlick't cub an ill-mannered, rude youngster

unmenseful untidy, ill-mannered (cf *raggelt*) (see *mense*)

unsneck unlatch

upbanks ascending, uphill (as opposed to *downbanks*, descending, downhill)

uppermer higher of two or more objects

Uppies and Downies Workington equivalent of the Eton Wall Game. This Easter Week mass football game consists of two teams, the *Uppies* (originally the *Uppey-gyaters*) and the *Downies* (originally the *Downey-gyaters*). There is no limit on the number of players, and traditionally the *Uppies* were miners and steelworkers, while the *Downies* were seamen and dock workers. The goals are the wall of Workington Hall and a capstan on the harbour side. First recorded in 1779, the 'game' is thought to have been played long before that date; fortunately

Urchin, urchan.

175

The Urswick Priapus Stone was once venerated as a fertility symbol.

for the property owners of the town, the action now mostly takes place on the Cloffocks, a marshy area of the River Derwent. Co-incidentally, a similar 'game', also called Uppies and Downies, is played on Christmas Day and New Year's Day in Kirkwall, Orkney.

upshot result, outcome *he went on t' spree an' t' upshot was they locked him up in t' blackhole* (qv) *o'er neet*

uptack reward for finding something

urchin, urchan hedgehog; the word 'hedgehog' is used in the far north of Cumbria (cf *erchin*, *orchan*) (OF *herichon*)

Urswick Priapus Stone limestone boulder now forming part of a wall not far from the medieval church in Great Urswick. Writing in 1801, the diarist William Fleming claimed that 'the inhabitants of Urswick were accustomed to dress [it] as a figure of Priapus on Midsummer Day, besmearing it with sheep salve (qv), tar, or butter, and covering it with rags of various dyes, the head ornamented with flowers'. Clearly it represented a potent form of fertility symbol and as such formed a part of a ritual to ensure a good harvest. Today it seems that its powers of fecundity are no longer required... (see **cult objects**)

us[1] me *give us a lile sup o' tea*

us[2] we *there's only us two here*

us[3] short for house, as in *Hogg-us, hen-us, peat-us* etc.

use money, use brass interest on a sum of money

U'stan (see *Oostan*)

V

Vagabond's friend.

vagabond's friend solomon's seal; used in the treatment of black eyes and bruises

varjus verjuice, liquor obtained from crab apples *as sour as crab varjus*

varneer, vannar very nearly, almost

varra very *it's dree* (qv) *work, varra*

ventersom' adventurous, rash

viewly, viewsome handsome, of good appearance, pleasing to look at

virgin-swarm swarm of bees from a swarm of the same season

voag repute *he's i' full voag, noo*

W

Waberthwaite Cumberland sausage the gastronomic equivalent of Perigord truffles or Beluga caviare! Made by the Woodall family in the traditional manner since 1828, this Cumbrian delicacy finds its way not only to the most exclusive London restaurants but also to the royal breakfast table in Buckingham Palace.

wad Also known as *black lead*, *graphite*, *cawke* and *plumbago*, this versatile mineral was once mined at Seathwaite in Borrowdale. Mentioned in a document dated 1555, it was originally used by local shepherds to *smit* (qv) their sheep, but later it was used in the glazing of pottery, the casting of cannon balls, the fixing of dye and as the raw material for pencils. It was even used, in powder form, as a medicine for upset stomachs! Such a valuable commodity brought high prices and it even entered into the **smuggling** (qv) trade, and at one time an armed guard had to be placed at the entrance to the mine. A single 'pipe', discovered in 1803, yielded *wad* worth £105,000, but after the 1830s output declined and the mines were closed.

waffey weak after an illness or with old age

wag by t' wo' clock without a case but having the pendulum exposed and swinging

Wainwright, Alfred, MBE The patron saint of fellwalkers. Having already gained a deep and lasting affection for the Lake District, Alfred Wainwright (1907–1991) moved in 1941 from his native Blackburn to Kendal where, in 1948, he became borough treasurer. His eight hand-lettered and cartographically superb guidebooks to the Lakeland Fells, completed between 1952 and 1974, were a labour of love and his lasting memorial. At his request, his ashes were scattered at Innominate Tarn on Haystacks, overlooking Buttermere. Since his death a 'Wainwright industry' has developed, ranging from walking boots to **Kendal mint cake** (qv). Would 'AW' have approved? The answer is probably 'yes' — if the profits went to one of his beloved animal charities.

wakes Although wakes are normally associated with Ireland, they were once common in Cumbria. Between death and interment, the corpse was watched by elderly people until the evening, and from then until the morning by young people. Bread, cheese, ale and tobacco were provided to fortify the mourners, and all mirrors in the room were covered with white cloths, since it was considered unlucky to see the reflection of a corpse in glass. (see *coze house*, *streek*, *touching the corpse*)

Walker, 'Wonderful' The Reverend Robert Walker (1709–1802) was one of those proud and independent dalesmen lionised by Wordsworth. Born at Seathwaite in Dunnerdale, the young Walker became a schoolmaster at Loweswater, where he took holy orders, and later became curate-cum-schoolmaster at Buttermere. Returning to Seathwaite in 1736 at a stipend of £5 per annum, he combined the post of curate and teacher with that of farmer, scribe, lawyer and village innkeeper! He educated and cared for his large family — he had twelve children — and although his stipend never exceeded £50 per year, when he died he left the remarkable sum of £2,000. (see *dales larnin'*)

wall head visible boundary built into a **drystone wall** (qv) to indicate ownership or responsibility for repair (see *dalt*)

wamly, wanty faint from hunger

wamp wasp

wampish irritable, tetchy

wandal slim, slender

wang, whang leather shoelace; a thong (I *thvengur*, shoelace)

wang tooth molar, back tooth

wankley weak, unstable *that barn's terrible wankley on its feet*

Wanla Walney

warda a week day, ie weekday as distinct from a Sunday (I *hver dag*, every day)

wark[1] an ache, commonly applied to the head, teeth, ear, belly etc. The term is common in most of Cumbria except the far west and the north, where *ache* is more common. (I *verkur*, an ache)

wark[2] work (see *Hard Wark Nivver Kilt Anybody*)

warm to beat *Ah'll warm tha backside for tha!*

warn to *bid* (qv) or give notice of a funeral

warts, cures for Folk medicine is awash with cures for warts. Among the Cumbrian remedies are: rubbing with a piece of stolen meat which is then buried in the ground; or two crossed straws in a

A wamp.

Wasdale Head Chapel is dedicated to St Olaf, the patron saint of Norway.

linen bag dropped at a crossroads — he who finds and opens the bag gets the warts, the previous sufferer being cured! A black slug rubbed on the wart and then impaled on a thorn hedge was commonly used, as was rubbing with the milky sap of the dandelion (see **pissibed**) or the leaves of **house leek** (qv). Warts could be **charmed**, and most Cumbrian **hiring fairs** (qv) were visited by **wart charmers** who would buy the warts for sixpence. (see also **folk cures**)

Wasdale Head Chapel   This tiny sixteenth century chapel at the head of the most Scandinavian of all Lakeland's dales, and overlooked by England's highest mountain and near its deepest lake, is appropriately enough dedicated to St Olaf, Norway's patron saint.

Washington, George (1732–1799) The first President of the United States had well-defined links with Cumbria. His grandmother Mildred Washington (*née* Warner) married George Gale, a Whitehaven merchant. She died in 1700/1 and is buried at St Nicholas's Church in Whitehaven. Her two sons by her first marriage, John and Augustine, were pupils at Appleby School, and later Augustine became the father of George Washington. George's two stepbrothers Lawrence Washington and Augustine Washington were, like their father, sent to Appleby School, and it seems that George, too, was destined for the same school, but the death of his father prevented this. The east window of Bowness Church, which almost certainly came from Cartmel Priory, contains the arms of a fifteenth century Washington, and from this the 'Stars and Stripes' of the American flag are said to be derived.

watch webs, watch weds children's game, sometimes called *Scotch* [sic] *and English*, now probably defunct. A line representing the Anglo-Scottish border was marked on the ground, and a pile of hats, coats, and jackets was deposited as *webs* or *weds* by both teams on each side of this mark. The object was to pillage the *webs*, but if caught, the *raider* was taken prisoner. The game began by *an Englisher* putting his or her foot over the Border and shouting *'Here's a leg in thy land, dry-bellied Scot!'* In this way did a children's game mimic the once-vicious Border raids.

wath ford. Several *waths* across the Solway Firth between England and Scotland were used regularly, indeed the name Solway is derived from 'Sul-wath'. Crossing the *waths* was not always uneventful; in 1216 the army of Alexander II, returning to Scotland after raiding Cumberland, was overwhelmed by the rapidly-advancing tide and, according to the legend, 1,900 men were drowned.

Watson, Richard (1737–1816) Bishop of Llandaff, was born at Heversham where his father was master of the grammar school.

After Trinity College, Cambridge, his self-confidence and unashamed 'string-pulling' secured for him the Chair of Chemistry at Cambridge — though he had never read a chemistry book in his life! Indeed, he almost succeeded in blowing himself up. His knowledge of Divinity was as limited as his knowledge of the sciences, but this small inadequacy did not prevent him lobbying for the Regius Chair of Divinity, and later the See of Llandaff was added to his 'glittering prizes'. His visits to his cathedral were very rare, and his interests were concentrated on breeding sheep on his estate at Calgarth, Cumbria, rather than shepherding his Welsh flock.

weat (see *wheaat*)

weather lore Among the many Cumbrian weather maxims are:
> If the owl calls twet, it will rain
>   the next day

and, from Cartmel:
> Gull, gull, fly to the sand
> There's always bad weather
> When you're on the land

and:
> If the ice at Martinmas bears
>   a duck
> The rest of the winter is slush
>   and muck

In Kendal, folk hedged their bets with:
> If the sun in red should set
> The next day surely will be wet.
> If the sun should set in grey
> The next will be a rainy day.

Generations of West Cumbrians have looked out westward across the Irish Sea; if the Isle of Man can be seen, it will rain within twelve hours; and if the island can't be seen — it's raining already! (see *Helm wind, Candlemas, bottom winds*)

wedder weather

weedlin' (see *recklin'*)

weemless spotless, without a fault (I *vammlaus*, spotless)

weemly easy, soft, quiet

well-dressing Although now largely confined to Derbyshire, the dressing of wells once took place in Cumbria. In 1894 on Maundy Thursday, W G Collingwood observed springs at Hawkshead Hill and Satterthwaite decorated with shards of broken crockery and coloured rags.

Wells, Benjamin well-known nineteenth century dancing master and **fiddler** (qv) much in demand for *merry neets* (qv). A C Gibson wrote a poem called *Ben Wells* which begins:

Kersmas (qv) *is hardly Kersmas noo!*

Nowte's left like what it used to be-
T' yall's nut what they used to brew-

An' t' fun's nut what we used to see-
T' lasses irn't hoaf sa smart,

For o' the'r fallal (qv) *hats an' veils*
An' music niver sturs yan's heart
Like 'T' Hunt's Up' played by oald Ben Wales [sic]

Welsh main cockfighting (qv) term for a *main* in which a given number of birds fought often to the death; the surviving half were pitted a second time, until only a quarter of the original number of birds remained — and so on, until two

birds were left and these two fought until the weaker one succumbed

welt to incline, to turn over on one side (I *velta*, to roll over)

wemmel, whemmel to turn a hollow vessel or dish upside down, to upset or overturn

wents, wentit on the point of turning sour *thunnery wedder* (qv) *wents milk*

weshin' t' barn's heead now an excuse for the proud father of a new-born child to *make merry* with his *marras* (qv), but traditionally the baby's head was literally washed with rum

West, Father Thomas Thomas West (1720–1779) was born in Scotland but settled at Tytup Hall, Furness. In 1774 he published his *Antiquities of Furness*, and four years later produced the first guidebook to the Lake District, the enormously popular *Guide to the Lakes in Cumberland, Westmorland and Lancashire*. Father West's great contribution to the interpretation of landscape was the idea of 'stations' or viewpoints to which the tourist was gently directed — he was a Jesuit priest and was probably influenced by the stations of the cross in Roman Catholic churches.

wether castrated *tup* (qv). The story is told of Ned Nelson of Gatesgarth, Buttermere, who had bred a *tup* which was expected to perform well with the *yowes* (qv). Expectations were sadly not fulfilled. Soon after, a friend of Ned's greeted him with 'Morning, Ned; fine weather', to which came the laconic response *'Nay, but it will be t'morra'*.

weyt　shallow dish, often made of sheepskin covering a wooden hoop. Used in *deeting* (qv) or winnowing grain.

whack　share, proportion *Ah've dun my whack an' paid my dues*

whang¹　(see *wang*)

whang²　a blow *he giv his lug* (qv) *sic a whang*

what for　retribution, punishment *Wait til tha fadder gits yam* (qv) — *he'll gi' thee what for!*

wheaat, weat　very young cockles (Morecambe Bay) (cf *hardbacks*)

whemmel　(see *wemmel*)

whezzle　to beat with a hazel rod

whick　living, alive, not dead (derived from 'quick') (N *kvikk*, lively, quickly)

whick dyke　growing hawthorn hedge, as distinct from a *dry dyke* (see also *liggers*)

whick'nin'　yeast added to baking bread

whig-whey　pleasant, refreshing drink, brewed for harvest workers, made by infusing mint or sage into buttermilk whey

while　until *Ah'll wait while three o'clock*

Whillimoor wang　a poor, skim-milk cheese, so tough that *wangs* (qv) could be made from it

whins　gorse, furze. Some farms had *whin dales* from which gorse was harvested, crushed and used for animal feed.

whintin　traditional name for a dark-coloured slate found in the Skiddaw area from which the famous *musical stones* (qv) in the Keswick museum are formed

whisht　silent, noiselessly *as whisht as mice*

white thorn　(see *hawthorn*)

Whitten　Whitehaven

whittle　knife (see *whittlegate*); also the dressing blade used in the shaping of roofing *slates¹* (qv) (see *dressing brake*)

whittlegate　Clergymen and schoolmasters had the privilege of dining — ie using his *whittle* (qv) — at each house in the parish in turn. In some instances the 'guests' stayed a week at each farm. The custom prevailed until 1864 and ceased with the death of the schoolmaster at Wasdale Head.

whooping cough, cures for Passing the sufferer under the belly of a donkey was quite common, but a variation, used in 1817 at Skelwith Bridge, near Ambleside, called for the patient to be tied to the back of a donkey with his nose to the tail, then the animal was walked over the bridge. Confinement in a cave or 'underground' excavation for several hours had its adherents, and William Fisher, a Barrow yeoman farmer, believed that rubbing the back and the soles of the feet with an infusion of rum and garlic was a 'sure cure'. (see **folk cures, tar machine**)

whye　heifer of any age up to three years old (I *kviga*, a heifer)

whyte　quite

wicks　maggots on a sheep

widdies　young willow shoots, osiers

This bizarre practice at Skelwith Bridge was believed to be a cure for whooping cough.

wife day, wiving when the mother of a new-born baby received her women friends and entertained them to tea (see *buttered sops*, *rum butter*)

wife-sale Hugh Walpole records the ficticious sale of a wife in his novel *Rogue Herries* (qv), but such sales did, in fact, occur. In 1812 William Fleming records in his diary the flight from Furness of a married lady and her lover; the pair were pursued by the aggrieved husband who, having caught up with the errant pair, sold his wife to her lover in Whitehaven market place 'for something less than one shilling'. In 1832 the annual register records a similar sale which occured in Carlisle, when one Joseph Thompson proposed selling his wife, Mary Anne,

for fifty shillings. Unfortunately there were no bidders, but eventually he agreed a sale with Henry Mears, who took Mary Anne for twenty shillings and a Newfoundland dog.

wiggs, whigs small buns made with wheat flour and caraway seeds, usually associated with Kendal and Hawkshead

Wigton (see *Throstle Nest*)

Wild Boar Fell traditionally the site of the slaying of the last wild boar by Sir Richard de Musgrave (died 1409). When his tomb in Kirkby Stephen Church was opened in the nineteenth century, the tusk of a wild boar was found. (see also **last wolf in England**)

Wild Dog of Ennerdale huge, smooth-coated beast which terrorised Ennerdale in the summer of

184

1810. This wily animal killed many sheep in the dale, usually under cover of darkness, and always selecting the plumpest sheep in the flock. All attempts to trap, shoot or poison the *girt dog* failed until, on the 12th September, he was cornered and shot. The carcass, weighing eight stones (50kg), was stuffed and exhibited in a Keswick museum.

Wilkinson, John A Cumbrian by birth, John Wilkinson (c1728–1808) was one of the great figures of the Industrial Revolution. Obsessed by iron, he owned ironworks in Shropshire, Staffordshire and Wales, as well as a furnace at Wil-

son House, Cartmel. Legend says that he built the world's first **iron boat** (qv). When he died in Shropshire in 1808, his body was placed in a wooden and lead coffin, and transported across the sands of Morecambe Bay for burial at his house at Castlehead in Cartmel. Sadly, the tide came in and John was buried for the first time. Eventually arriving at Castlehead, the iron coffin he had requested was found to be too small, so John was buried a second time in a temporary grave. When the larger iron coffin arrived, the new grave hit solid rock — so once more John was reburied for a third time, until

The Wild Dog of Ennerdale.

A willy-wicket.

a deeper grave could be excavated. At last the grave in the grounds of Castlehead was prepared and John Wilkinson, ironmaster, was laid to rest — but not for long. In 1828 the house was sold and the new owners, not wishing to have the previous owner in their garden, had John removed to Lindale Church. The exact location remains a secret.

willsta? will you?

Willy o' th' Hollins also known as William Gibson (1720–1791) of Cartmel Fell, was a self-taught mathematical genius. He taught himself to read and write, but his understanding of mathematics, geometry, algebra, trigonometry, land surveying, navigation and astronomy was nothing short of miraculous. For forty years he ran a small school for 8 to 10 gentlemen on his farm, and among his pupils was **John Barrow** (qv) of Ulverston, later to distinguish himself in the Admiralty. (see *dales larnin'*)

willy-wicket　sandpiper

Windermere Ferry　(see Crier of Claife)

wine berries　redcurrants

winklin'　youngest pig in a litter (see *recklin'*)

win' raw　row of peats or ridge of hay drying in the wind or sun (derived from 'wind row')

winter　to survive through the winter; *he sends his hogs to Wanla* (qv) *to winter*; a common greeting heard in the spring is *Hasta* (qv) *wintered well?*

wise man, wise woman　local people who had developed a reputation for healing. A visit to a wise man or woman involved some form of psychosomatic medicine such as spells or potions. The Cumbria Record Office has a number of 'commonplace books' of these untutored medicos, whose methods were somewhat unconventional. (see **folk cures**)

wisp, wusp　·handful of straw placed in **clogs** (qv) to keep the feet warm and insulate them from the damp earth

witchcraft　died hard in Cumbria. A page purporting to come from the Register of Deaths in Lamplugh parish from January 1658 to 1663 includes:

Frightened to death by fairies　3
Bewitched　4
*Old women drowned upon
　trial by witchcraft*　3

*Led into a horse pond by
　a will o' the wisp*　1

The commonplace book of an eighteenth century Troutbeck farmer, Christopher Birkett, contains a spell to cure bewitched cattle which calls for the hair from the animals to be roasted in a fire and ends with the words '... when the ashes are cold, bury them in the ground towards that quarter of heaven where the suspected witch lives'. Regrettably, the commonplace book does not give the success rate of such methods. (see **Baynes, Mary**, *bor-tree*, *dobby stones*, *evil eye*, Scot, Michael, wise man, wise woman)

witch-wand　twig of the mountain ash (see *rowan*)

wither, whidder　to tremble, to quiver, to shudder, to shake

wiving　(see *wife day*)

wolf　(see **last wolf in England**)

wolfen　(see *wulf*)

woo', oo', ooa　dialect variations of the word wool. Ellwood reports the following conversation between a farmer and a wool dealer:
Dealer: Oo? (wool?)
Farmer: Aye, oo (yes, wool)
Dealer: Aw oo? (all wool?)
Farmer: Aye, aw oo (yes, all wool)
Dealer: Aw ya oo? (all one wool?)
Farmer: Aye, aw ya oo (Yes, all one wool, ie wool from the same clipping)

Wordsworth, William　(1770–1850) born in comfortable surroundings in Cockermouth, where his father was land agent to Sir James Lowther. Much has been written of his boyhood in Hawkshead and Colthouse, his education at Cambridge and his most productive period at Dove Cottage, Grasmere, between 1799 and 1808. He is, without doubt, the High Priest of the Romantic Movement. His political development ranged from an enthusiastic supporter of the French Revolution in

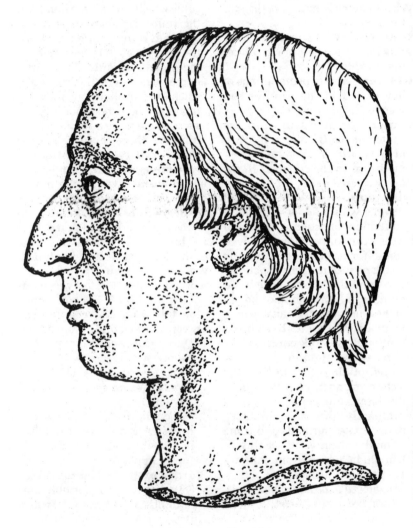

William Wordsworth.

Wrestler slates interlock like Cumberland and Westmorland wrestlers.

his youth, to a High Tory in old age when he objected to the railways tempting 'the humbler classes to leave their homes' and venture into his mountain fastness — yet he enquired of Charles Lloyd which railway company he should invest in! His reputation amongst the local dalesmen was not as exhalted as in some quarters; to them his poetry was *'aw reet eneuf, but queer stuff, varra'* (qv) and, as one of them acknowledged wisely: *'Miss Dorothy did best part o' putting his poetry togidder. He let it fa' and she cam efter and gathered it oop for him, ye kna'*. But in many ways it is the human side of Wordsworth rather than the venerated poet laureate which is most appealing; the youngster roaming the fells with

pieces of Ann Tyson's *haver bread* (qv) and cheese in his pockets, the schoolboy nutting in the Furness woods or skating on the frozen tarns, or swimming in Esthwaite — all experiences which engendered in him a deep and lasting love for his native countryside. His grave at Grasmere is surrounded by the Lakeland fells; it is marked by a simple tombstone but, as was said of Sir Christopher Wren: *Si Monumentum Requiris, Circumspice.*

worrit to harras or perplex; also used of a person who frets or worries *she's nobbut a girt worrit*

worthings ancient name for manure; the term is used in the medieval documents of Furness Abbey

wrecking The salvaging of timber from wrecked vessels on the

Cumberland and Westmorland wrestling is an integral part of Cumbrian folklife.

treacherous coastline of Cumbria was once quite common. On Biggar Bank, on the west coast of Walney Island, it is said that a donkey was hobbled and a lantern placed around its neck to deliberately attract vessels onto the shore. One story relates how news of a wreck reached Walney Chapel as a service was in progress; the congregation left immediately to claim the pickings, followed by the vicar who was heard to shout *'Hod still a lile bit, theer, let's o' hev a fair start'*.

wrecklin' (see *recklin'*)

wrestler slates slates on the ridge of a roof which are so designed as to interlock with their neighbours

wrestling Far removed from the 'grunt and groan' sessions once seen on television, **Cumberland and Westmorland wrestling** is an integral element of the area's folk culture, as much a part of things as *rum butter* and *tatie-pot*. The skill depends not on brute force but on balance and agility as the competitors *tek hod* by clasping hands around each other's backs. To many, the names of the moves — *hypeing, haming, cross buttocking* and *hankering* — are a foreign language, but to Cumbrians they are as familiar as their own dialect. There are remarkable similarities with *glima*, the Icelandic national sport, and this has led to a belief that this form of wrestling was introduced into both areas by people of Scandinavian Viking extraction. However, it should also be noted that a similar type of wrestling takes place in the 'Celtic' areas of Wales, Cornwall and Brittany. (see also *cross buttock, dog fall, hankering the heel, hype,* Steadman, George)

Written Rock of Gelt West of the Roman fort at Birdoswald on Hadrian's Wall is a sandstone quarry once used by Roman troops. Here on the banks of the River Gelt, these Roman quarrymen have left a number of inscriptions. Not far away is Pigeon Crag where men of the Sixth Legion have written their names.

Wukkit'n Workington

wulf, wolfen to eat voraciously *Give over* (qv) *wulfen thi dinner!* (cf *gollop*)

Y

ya, yan one *thoo'll be gitten wed ya day*

yad mare *she was a yad fit for a king*

yaddle (cf *addle*, *eddle*)

yak oak (I, N *eik*, oak)

yaker acre

yakkeren acorn

yal, yel ale

yalla yowderin' yellowhammer

yam, yem home (N *heim*, home)

yammer to talk or to grumble in a rambling manner *what's ta yammering on aboot?*

yananudder, yananither one another

yan on twa an' twa on yan the drystone waller's (qv) maxim, meaning that one stone is placed on two lower stones and two placed on one to form a bonding

yance once; *yance oor* means at one time, formerly

yar¹ hare

yar² harsh, sour (north Cumbria)

yark to beat with a stick, the harshest of blows *I'll yark tha hide!* (I *thjarka*, to belabour, quarrel)

yat gate

yebby (see *yebby*)

yedder severe blow with a switch; also a long rod used in hedging

yerb pudding (see *Easterledge pudding*)

yerdfasts large, immovable boulders on or near the surface

yerls, yarls (see *arles*)

yew trees Tradition maintains that yew trees were grown to supply the wood for longbows and, in order to prevent animals grazing on the poisonous berries, they were planted in enclosed churchyards. Certainly Cumbria has its share of churchyard yews, but at High Yewdale, near Coniston, an

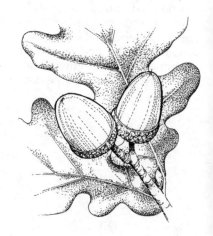

Yakkerens.

192

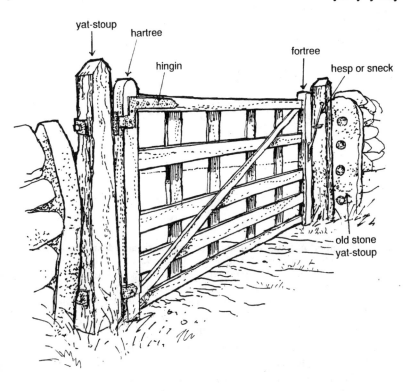

A five-barred yat. On the right, an old stone 'yat-stoup' has holes in which 'gap rails' were once positioned.

eighteenth century farmer supposedly planted a yew each time his wife bore a child. There are fifteen trees in a straight line opposite the farmhouse — arboreal evidence of the couple's fecundity.

yoller to halloo

yon that, those

Yorkshire Dales National Park Part of the Dales National Park lies, perversely, within the County of Cumbria. The areas around Sedbergh and Dent were part of Yorkshire until the local government boundary changes in 1974.

youlet (see *hullet*)

yowe, yow ewe, female sheep (see *gimmer*)

yower, yewer udder of an animal (I *jugur*, N *jur*, udder)

yowl to howl

yule log traditionally lit on Christmas Eve, if possible using a fragment of the previous yule log, since this was regarded as a potent good luck charm

yuly-yuly call to bring geese together (cf *giss-giss-giss*)

Bibliography

KEY:
CW1   Cumberland and Westmorland Antiquarian and Archaeological
       Society Transactions, Old Series, 1866–1900
CW2   Cumberland and Westmorland Antiquarian and Archaeological
       Society Transactions, New Series, 1901–present
THSLC Transactions of the Historic Society of Lancashire and Cheshire

Allen, P, *The Old Galleries of Cumbria*, 1984
Armistead, W, *Tales and Legends of the English Lakes*, 1891
Armitt M L, *Rydal*, 1916
    The Church at Grasmere, a History, 1912
Barber, H, *Furness and Cartmel Notes*, 1894
Blake, B, *The Solway Firth*, 1955
Bott, G, *Keswick: The Story of a Lake District Town*, 1994
Bragg, M, *Land of the Lakes*, 1983
    Speak for England, 1976
Budworth, J, *A Fortnight's Ramble to the Lakes*, 1795
Buntin, T F, *Life in Langdale*, 1993
Carruthers, F J, *Lore of the Lake Country*, 1975
    Around the Lakeland Hills, 1976
Clarke, J, *A Survey of the Lakes of Cumberland, Westmorland and
    Lancashire*, 1787
Collingwood, W G, *Lake District History*, 1925
    The Lake Counties, 1902 (new edition, 1988)
Cowper, H S, *Hawkshead*, 1899
    On Some Obsolete or Semi-Obsolete Appliances, CW1, vol 13
    Illustrations of Old Fashions and Obsolete Contrivances, CW1, vol 15

Cumbria Federation of Women's Institutes, *Cumbria Within Living Memory*, 1994

Denwood, J M, *Oor Mak o' Toak*, 1946

Denwood, M, and Thompson, T W, *A Lafter o'Farleys in t' Dialect o' Lakeland, 1760-1945*, 1950

Dickinson, W, *A Glossary of Words and Phrases pertaining to the Dialect of Cumberland*, 1878

Dilley, R S, *Some Words Used in the Agrarian History of Cumberland*, CW2, vol, 70, 1970

Ellwood, T, *Lakeland and Iceland, being a Glossary of Words in the Dialect of Cumberland, Westmorland and North Lancashire which seem allied or identical with the Icelandic or Norse*, 1895 (reprint, 1995)

Mountain Sheep, their origins and markings, CW1, vol 15

Fell, J, *The Guides over the Kent and Leven Sands*, CW1, vol 7

Ferguson, R, *The Northmen in Cumberland and Westmorland*, 1856

Ffinch, M, *Portrait of Kendal and the Kent*, 1983

Portrait of Penrith and the East Fellside, 1985

Portrait of the Howgills and the Upper Eden Valley, 1982

Fisher, W, *Manuscript Diary and Account Book, 1811–1859*, Cumbria Record Office, Barrow

Fleming, W, *Manuscript Diary and Commonplace Book, 1798-1819*, microfilm, Barrow Public Library

Gell, W, *A Tour in the Lakes made in 1797* (ed W Rollinson), 1968

Gibson, A C, *The Old Man*, 1857

Ancient Customs and Superstitions in Cumberland, THSLC, vol 10, Old Series, 1857-8

The Folk Speech of Cumberland and Westmorland and Some Districts Adjacent, 1868

Gough, J, *The Manners and Customs of Westmorland and adjoining parts of Cumberland, Lancashire and Yorkshire*, 1812 (reprinted, 1827)

Hodgson, J, *Westmorland As It Was*, reprinted in the *Lonsdale Magazine*, vol 3, 1822, with additional notes by J Briggs

Jollie, F, *Sketch of Cumberland Manners and Customs*, 1811

Journal of the Lake District Dialect Society (Press Secretary: Mrs J Scott-Smith, Gale View, Main Street, Shap, via Penrith, Cumbria CA10 3NH)

Kendall, W B, *William Barrow Kendall's Forness* [sic] *Word Book, begun at Salthouse in the Year 1867*, Manuscript, Cumbria Record Office, Barrow

Kirkby, B, *Lakeland Words*, 1898 (reprint 1975)

Lefebure, M, *Cumberland Heritage*, 1970

Linton, E Lynn, *The Lake Country*, 1864

McIntire, W T, *Lakeland and the Borders of Long Ago*, 1949

Marshall, F, *Charlotte Deans, 1768-1859*, 1984

Marshall, J D, *Old Lakeland*, 1971
  Portrait of Cumbria, 1981

Martineau, H, *A Description of the English Lakes*, 1858

Morris, J P, *A Glossary of the Words and Phrases of Furness*, 1869

Nicholson, N, *Cumberland and Westmorland*, 1949
  Portrait of the Lakes, 1963
  The Lakers, 1955
  Collected Poems (ed Neil Curry), 1994
  Lakeland, A Prose Anthology, 1991
  Wednesday Early Closing, 1975
  Greater Lakeland, 1969

Nicolson, J, and Burn, R, *The History and Antiquities of the Counties of Cumberland and Westmorland*, 1777

Nodal, J H, and Milner, G, *A Glossary of the Dialect of Lancashire*, 1875

Peacock, R B, *A Glossary of the Dialect of the Hundred of Lonsdale North and South of the Sands*, 1869

Richardson, J, *Old Customs and Usages of the Lake District*, Trans of the Cumberland and Westmorland Association for the Advancement of Literature and Science, 1876

Richardson, S, *Tales of a Lakeland Gypsy*, 1996

Robinson, C, *Sand Pilot of Morecambe Bay*, 1980

Rollinson, W, *A History of Man in the Lake District*, 1967
  A History of Cumberland and Westmorland, 2nd edn 1996
  The Lake District: Life and Traditions, 1996

Rowling, M, *The Folklore of the Lake District*, 1976

Sands, R, *Portrait of the Wordsworth Country*, 1984

Scott, D, *Bygone Cumberland and Westmorland*, 1899

Scott, H S, *A Westmorland Village*, 1904

Stockdale, J, *Annals of Cartmel*, 1872

Sullivan, J, *Cumberland and Westmorland, Ancient and Modern*, 1857

Taylor, S, *A Flookburgh Glossary*, CW2, vol 27, 1927
    Cartmel People and Priory, 1955
Upton, C, Sanderson, S, and Widdowson, J D A, *Word Maps: A Dialect Atlas of England*, 1987
Upton, C, and Widdowson, J D A, *An Atlas of English Dialects*, 1996
Ward, E M, *Days in Lakeland*, 1929
Westmorland Notebook, Vol 1, 1888-9
Wright, J (ed), *The English Dialect Dictionary* (6 vols, 1898-1905)
Wright, P, *Cumbrian Dialect*, 1979